Knitorama

D1314071

fantastic knitting creations

glamorous things to wear

fabulous non-essentials

knitted decorations

Knitorama

Rachael Matthews

MQP

MQ Publications Limited

12 The Ivories, 6–8 Northampton Street

London, N1 2HY, UK

Tel: +44 (0) 20 7359 2244

Fax: +44 (0) 20 7359 1616

49 West 24th Street, 8th Floor

New York, NY 10010, USA

Tel: 212-223-6320

E-mail: mail@mqpublications.com

Web site: www.mqpublications.com

Copyright © 2005 MQ Publications Limited

Text copyright © 2005 Rachael Matthews

EDITOR: Katy Bevan

PHOTOGRAPHY: Angus Leadley Brown

DESIGN: C-B Design

All rights reserved. No part of this publication may be reproduced or transmitted in any
form or by any means, electronic or mechanical, including photocopy, recording, or any
information storage and retrieval system now known or to be invented without permission
in writing from the publishers. The author and publisher disclaim all responsibility for
any liability, loss, or risk, personal or otherwise, which is incurred as a consequence,
directly or indirectly, of the use and application of any of the contents of this book.

ISBN: 1-59223-345-7

Printed and bound in Europe

1 2 3 4 5 08 07 06 05 04

Contents

✻ Have some fun, and remember, it's only yarn!

Yarn foreword

It brings me much happiness to write a few words of introduction
for my lovely friend Rachael's new knitting book.

A few weeks ago I paid a visit to the magical studio where Rachael, and her ever-smiling assistant Annie, showed me the ingenious designs that are brought to you with all their hard, loving work. They will explode at you from the following pages. I skipped away full of hard-water Yorkshire Tea, with sunshine in my soul, lots of happy thoughts about knitting, and feeling extremely proud to know someone who was even attempting to write a pattern for flying ducks.

We were all beginners once, and if this is the first knitting book you have ever held in your hands, don't be scared—Rachael will show you the easy stuff until you are ready to tackle the "bitches," as she affectionately calls them.

Rachael learned how to knit and make her own designs when she was a teenager, but she was quite grown-up when I met her. We knew instantly that we would like each other and become friends because of knitting. We turned our love for knitting into social events so that even the more isolated of our knitter friends could get out and have fun. Our roaming Cast Off club grew like a giant cable, knit of new intertwining relations between all kinds of knitters from all walks and stages of life. They just wanted to take their knitting with them wherever they went. For all of us, knitting goes hand in knitted mitten with dancing at the disco, drinking a beer or two, going shopping, a day at the seaside, a ride on the subway, waiting in line, or marching in protest against the war.

Only able to afford the occasional trip to the yarn section of a department store, many of us found those excellent odd balls, wound by old ladies in thrift stores, without a pattern in sight. Knitted spontaneously, they were sometimes useful, but always hilarious. There was no object in life that could not be knitted.

Today Rachael runs the club with imagination and gusto, but Cast Off spin-offs have meant that knitting clubs are meeting on their own in cinemas and on buses all over the world, which is a good thing really, because Rachael needed some time off to write this book.

Knitting usually starts at home, often with mother or grandmother, and this book will help you to knit around your abode. Whether your home is a trailer or a country mansion you can still love it, clean its windows in woolly, soapy style, cook knitted vegetables and serve crafted cakes for your dinner party, wash up afterwards in your stitched sink, or just lounge lazily around, feeling sexy in a knitted garter, while sipping your pint of crocheted stout and thinking about your next knitting adventure.

It's a good time for Rachael to connect knitting back to its humble, domestic origins. We were aware of a media frenzy about knitting, especially because we were always being interviewed, and it was quite exhausting. Journalists always wanted to pepper their articles with stories of celebrities knitting in Hollywood, as if it was a phenomenon—celebrities are people after all—and, as we discovered, lots of people happen to like knitting. Feminism often creeps into these discussions, but we've always encouraged and welcomed the many boys who love to knit, and Rachael's designed this book with knitting-men in mind too.

As Rachael always says, knitting is about love. There's nothing more special than a gift lovingly knitted for you by your lover. OK, so often the sweater is a bit uncomfortable, and he might resent wearing it but Rachael's thought of that and designed a sweater that his hot water bottle can wear instead. It's beautiful and when he's away on his Arctic expeditions, it will remind him of you. And guys, you don't have to go shopping for sexy lingerie anymore—now that there's a naughty nightdress to knit—and you can impress her by making a practical dishcloth while you're at it.

Knitting is for friends of a platonic nature too. It takes a long time to make a cardigan on your own, but if everyone does a square you can knit one together in a day. Above all, through knitting, we all get closer to those relations who we loved first of all—our moms.

Back in the cozy but industrious atmosphere of Rachael's colorful studio, the revolutionary designs made me fall about laughing, the gorgeous models made me fall in love, the patterns actually made sense for a change, but what hit me most of all was that this book will inspire you, the reader, to knit what you want.

So throw that knitted hand grenade at your TV and do something more interesting instead. Actually knitting and watching telly is quite a good combination...especially with a lovely cup of Yorkshire Tea.

With love,
Amy Plant
London, June 2005

Knitting in public

This is my friend Amy, with her basket of wool, waiting to board a train at Liverpool Street station in London. Amy and I formed Cast Off in 2001. At that time, we didn't really know any other knitters but we had friends that wanted to learn. We loved journeys, going out, meeting new people, and knitting.

What I love about London is that things change. There are always new places to take your knitting. We wanted Cast Off to meet in a different place each time. That way we could constantly teach new people to knit and our club would grow. The men and women that came to our club were such colorful, creative, characters. Seeing them all chatting on the subway with busy fingers, and yarn everywhere, was the kind of image I'd been looking for the whole ten years I had lived in London. Creative people are everywhere, but it is hard to notice them when their creativity is hidden in the home. Knitting is one of the few crafts that you can take anywhere, so there are endless possibilities.

Knitters are characteristically fidgets. If you can't sit still on the bus or through films, or you hate waiting in line or sitting through boring meetings, then knitting is the craft for you. Knitting requires concentration, at first, but with practice you can soon knit and chat and watch TV. Once you can knit without looking, you can knit anywhere because it's such a portable hobby. Historically, knitting was always done in public, because it was done as often as possible. In the days when women were working purely in the home, knitting was a job that filled spare minutes and created extra income—the original "pin money."

Organising a knitting circle in public is relatively easy. You can't really get in trouble for group knitting because you are "just knitting." You can use the

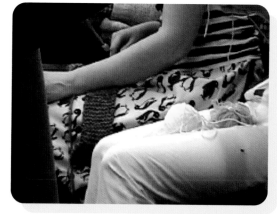

preconception that knitting is a harmless pastime practiced by old ladies to your advantage. You will always appear peaceful and non-threatening when you are knitting, so use this image to make the most of public spaces that you wouldn't normally use. Some public spaces have terrible lighting. Cast Off members recommend wearing mining lamps, which consist of a lamp on an elastic headband. The light points down on your knitting, or on each other, depending on where you are looking.

Getting in trouble can also be fun. Cast Off was once thrown out of a posh hotel bar for knitting. The headwaiter said that knitting was something that should be done at home. The trouble made the evening the funniest night out we had ever had.

Knitting in public really inspires people to converse with you. This can feel a bit scary, you might be knitting on the bus, off in your own dream world, and a stranger may give you funny looks. Never assume they think you are strange—the likelihood is that you are evoking memories in them, and they are thinking of their grandmother or a teddy bear's scarf they made once at school. There is magic in creativity, and anyone interested in knitting has a story to tell and a spark to ignite your friendship. Carry an extra pair of needles and some yarn in your bag just in case someone wants to relearn.

Once you are addicted to knitting you will have to plan your life accordingly. Experienced knitters will tell you they have hoards of yarn they might never use, but may need for emergencies. Worst-case scenarios would be family gatherings at Christmas, with no knitting to do and no yarn store for miles, or finding yourself stuck in a traffic jam for hours without your knitting. Airplanes are still a difficult issue. There have been a series of tricky rules about taking knitting needles on airplanes. Crafters are not terrorists, but we are practical, and we are allowed to knit with pencils or straws.

and they are all knitted!

cooking and knitting recipes

knitting hints and tips

How to Knit

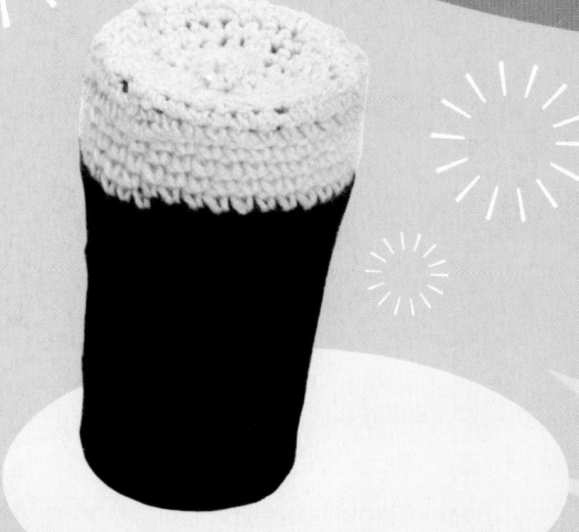

relaxing crochet projects

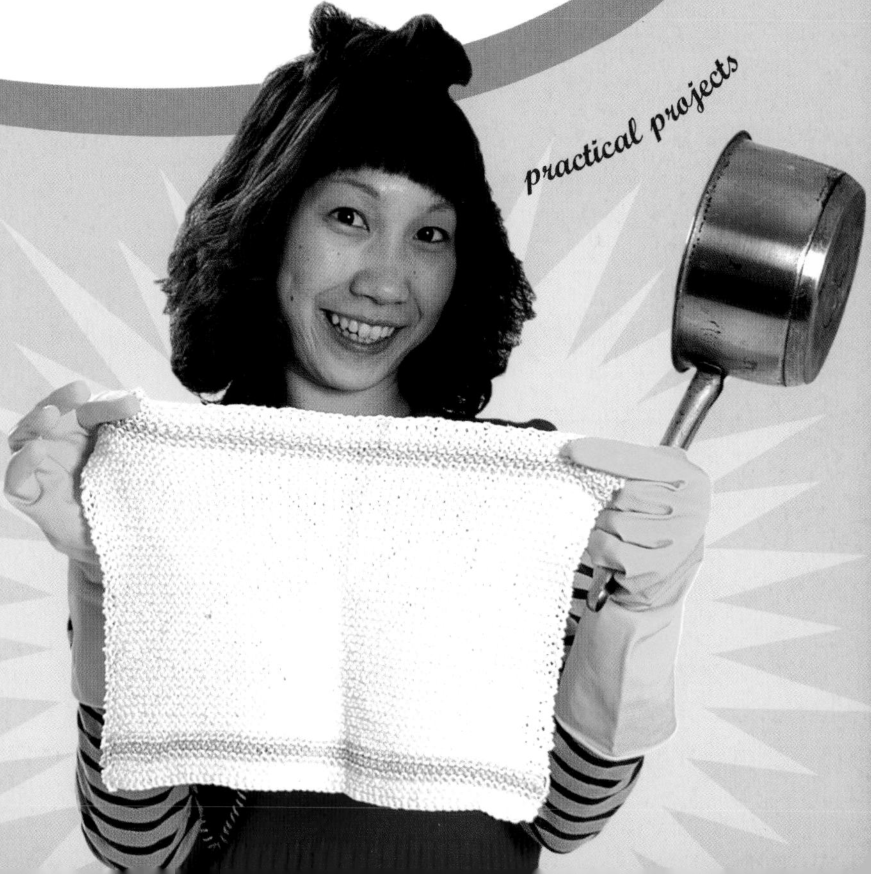

practical projects

Getting started

If you've never knitted before or you are relearning, it really helps to have a friend to knit with. This book will show you easy step-by-step guides, but sometimes beginners make funny tangles and might need help. There is usually a fluent knitter somewhere, in your family, at work, or maybe the lady in the local store. A knitter never minds untangling!

✳ A messy tangle of yarn can happen...

The basic principle of knitting is that you have a row of stitches, which you pass from the left-hand needle to the right-hand needle and, while doing this, you put a new loop through each stitch, making the knitting grow longer. If you unravel a piece of knitting, you will see a row of loops, and as you pull the thread out, these loops disappear into another row of loops from the row below.

When teaching a beginner to knit, I advise that they first find a ball of yarn that they find attractive. Learning to knit requires a bit of perseverance, and it helps if you can bond with your ball. Go to your local yarn store, and potter around, picking up yarn that you like the look of. Your favorite color and texture will change depending on your mood, the weather, or someone you have on your mind. Rub the yarn on your face, smell it too. If it feels good and the ideas are forming, then buy it. You can pick up some really interesting yarns on the Internet. There are spinners out there who work with natural organic fibers and dyes, and many types of wool. There is a worldwide online woolly community, so just start surfing!

Buying yarn can be expensive. Knitting is no longer economically viable as far as making clothes goes. It's cheaper and quicker to go out and buy a sweater from your local chain store, but it's unlikely you will enjoy it as much as a handmade one. The value of a hand-knitted item is far higher in emotion and stories than anything made by a machine in a far off place you might never go to.

You can knit with anything, so long as it is very long, fibrous, and doesn't snap. If you are following a pattern for a large project it is advisable to use the yarn they suggest. This can become expensive, but some yarn stores will hold the full amount for you so you can buy a ball every time you need one. For little projects, you can collect yarn in your own time. Look for yarn and needles at garage sales or thrift stores, or ask your relations to empty their cupboards and blanket boxes.

Keeping your yarn

Keep your favorite yarn out on display for inspiration, but keep other yarns somewhere moth free, preferably in paper bags and with cedarwood or lavender to keep them smelling fresh.

Skeins

Sometimes yarn comes in a skein rather than a ball. The yarn is dyed in a skein to get an even color. There is a tool called a niddy noddy, onto which you place your skein, and then wind it from that into a ball. It's not easy to buy a niddy noddy these days, but you can use the back of a chair. The fastest and most fun way to wind a skein into a ball is for someone else to stretch the skein over their hands, switch the music on, and you wind the ball as fast as you can. Keep two or three fingers over the yarn as you wind it to stop it being wound too tight and stretching the yarn. The skein holder has to move their hands in quite a groovy way to keep up with your speed, and you can have a little dance.

Winding up a bobbin

When working with more than one color, intarsia, you can get in a terrible tangle. Using a whole ball of yarn for each color makes it worse—especially if you have a cat—so make smaller balls, called bobbins or spools. Using the thumb and little finger, wrap the yarn around in a figure of eight until you think you have enough. Break off the yarn from the main ball, and wrap it around the middle of the bobbin to secure it. Find the yarn in the center of the bobbin and attach it to your knitting by tying a little knot. You can buy plastic bobbin reels, which are easier, or you can be traditional and use jam jars, but this is more difficult when knitting with six colors on the bus.

✳ *Nice neat balls of yarn.*

Winding bobbins and skeins

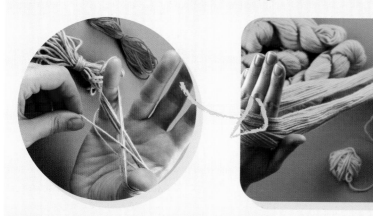

Winding a bobbin

Using your little finger and thumb, wrap the yarn in a figure of eight. Secure around the center, and use the yarn from the center of the bobbin first to save tangles.

Winding a skein

Get a friend to hold the open skein on their hands while you roll it into a ball. The back of a chair will do, but is not as sociable.

Yarn types

You can knit almost anything, as long as it is a continuous strip or string of material. There are many beautiful yarns to buy in yarn stores, but yarn in your stash may also have been passed on by other knitters. Great yarn is also often available in thrift stores and in your grandmother's bottom drawer.

There are many different types of yarn. Patterns in this book tell you the preferred type of yarn for the project, but I advise you to experiment with what you find.

Found yarns can be difficult to identify if they have no label. A good way to discover what it is made from is to do a flame test. Flame tests are dangerous because they involve fire.

Do it outside and away from anything flammable, please. You do not need to set fire to the whole ball. Take a little bit of yarn and light it. Observe what happens, and study the ash.

Fiber	Type of flame	Type of smoke	Type of ash or other residue	Smell given off
Cotton Linen Viscose rayon Jute	Burns fast with a yellow flame	Gray	Soft feathery ash, and not much of it. If it is crease resistant a blackened ash skeleton is left	Bit like burning paper, but if it's crease resistant it has overtones of rotten fish
Animal fibers Wool from sheep Silk from silkworm	Burns slowly with an irregular, spluttery flame	Gray	Brittle spongy black stuff	Smells a bit like when you accidentally set fire to your hair
Man-made fibers Nylon and polyester	A fast yellow flame where the yarn melts	Gray	Forms a black or brown bead that is quite hard	Sometimes smells of cooked celery or can smell sweeter like hot aromatic oil
Acrylic	Burns dangerously fast with a luminous flame	Thick black choking smoke	Forms a solid black lump	Smells worse than a burning tyre on tarmac

Yarn comes from lots of different places...

Cotton comes from a plant, as does linen.

Cashmere comes from the underbelly of the Himalayan goat.

Kid mohair is from a goat's first shearing.

Angora comes from rabbits.

The silk worm makes silk for its cocoon before becoming a moth.

Label information

Check shade and dye lot numbers match.

Make up and washing intructions.

100g
BS 984:76
MADE in UK
THE MILL®
Yorkshire BD12 1PR

Shade Dye
1145 11077

BIG SOFTY

100% WOOL

4mm 304metres

Weight and country of origin.

Tools for the job

Knitting needles and crochet hooks, or pins as they used to be called, come in all different sizes and are usually made from plastic, bamboo, metal, or wood.

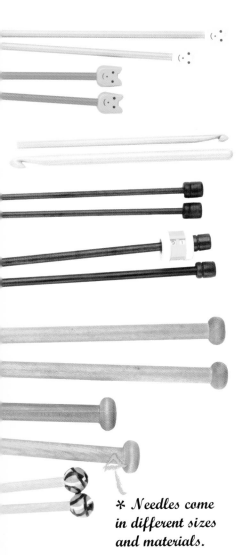

✻ *Needles come in different sizes and materials.*

Metal needles make the best clicking sound and are really strong. They will bend but never snap and can be dangerous if used as a weapon. Metal is not good for anyone suffering from repetitive strain injuries.

Bamboo needles have the quietest clicking and are the lightest of all the needles. They are good for long distance knitting and repetitive strain injuries. They do snap, however, so don't sit on them.

Plastic needles are good all round needles. Medium clicking, fairly light, and they can come in lovely colors. The thinner needles are fragile though and can break if your tension is too tight. Modern plastic needles can taste a bit salty, so avoid chewing the ends.

Wooden needles have a mellow clicking sound and look lovely. They are medium to heavy weight, and quite strong. If they are not finished properly they can splinter, but you can polish them with beeswax to speed your knitting, and they become really smooth with use.

Tortoise shell and ivory needles are very rare. Thank goodness they don't make needles out of these materials any more, but they do turn up from time to time in thrift stores. If you do find any, take good care of them.

Needle length Needles come in all different lengths. When planning your project, think about how many stitches you will have and whether you will need long needles.

Circular knitting is done either on four double-ended needles or on circular needles, which are flexible, and can come in different lengths. Knitting in the round means you can avoid seams.

Cable needles are tiny double-ended needles used for holding a small amount of stitches in cabling. Sometimes they have a dip in the middle to hold the stitches on.

Stitch holders are like a big safety pin and are used for holding stitches that will be knitted later. If you don't have one you can thread a long piece of yarn through the stitches.

*✳ Kinked cable
needles don't fall out
of your work so often.*

*✳ Stitch holders and
needle gauges are
useful extras.*

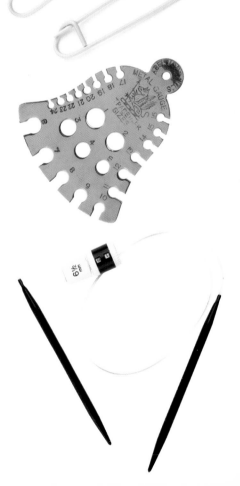

Little sewing scissors need to be small and sharp—tie them to your knitting bag. Look after them and don't let your friends and family use them for manicures or they will be ruined.

A needle gauge is vital if you are collecting old needles where the sizes have worn off, or if they are sized in pre-metric days. English, imperial, metric, and American sizes are all different and it can be very confusing.

Crochet hooks are useful for picking up dropped stitches—and for crochet of course.

A little graph paper notebook is handy for counting stitches, designing patterns, or for visualizing a written pattern you don't understand. Use one square for each stitch. Moleskin sketch books are the best because they have a pocket in the back to keep things in.

Row counters go on the end of the needle and you change the number every row. They look endearing on the end of a needle.

Point protectors are little flexible, plastic things that you put on the sharp end of your needles when your knitting is in transit. They stop the stitches falling off and stop the needles poking through your handbag and stabbing someone as you brush past them.

Yarn needles are for sewing up your knitting. They have an extra large eye, and are easy to loose, so put them somewhere safe.

*✳ These flexible
needles have a row
counter and point
protectors built in.*

Basics

There are many ways to cast on. Methods change depending on which part of the world you come from. Here are three common methods, all of which start with the slipknot.

Making a slipknot

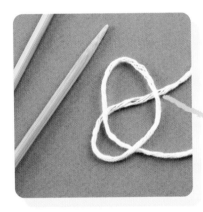

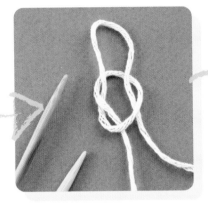

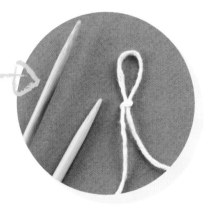

1 The slipknot is the first stitch of your knitting. Make a loop by passing the right side of the yarn over the left.

2 Take the tail end and make a second loop through the center of the first loop.

3 Pull the tail end to secure the slipknot.

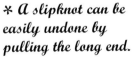

4 Place the slipknot on the left needle. This will count as your first stitch.

✳ A slipknot can be easily undone by pulling the long end.

Cast on with two needles

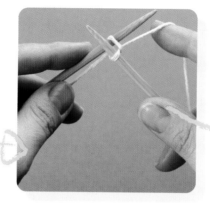

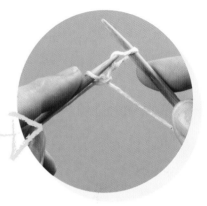

1 Now put your left needle (or right if you are left-handed) through the slipknot and pull it tight, but not too tight. Now you are ready to cast on. Put the right needle into the loop so that it passes under the left-hand needle. You are forming a cross with your needles and the right-hand needle is at the back.

2 Wrap the yarn around the back needle coming between the needles. Take the yarn through the first loop with the back needle. This is your new stitch.

3 Put this new stitch on the left needle, next to the previous stitch.

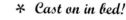

4 Now you have two stitches. Repeat by putting the right-hand needle into the last stitch on the left-hand needle, and keep making stitches until you have enough.

* Cast on in bed!

Casting on thumb method

This is casting on using one needle and your thumb. Use the short end of the yarn, and make it at least three times as long as your required cast on edge.

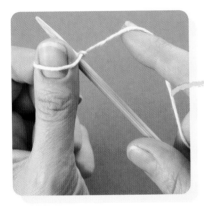

1 Make a slipknot please! (see page 20.)

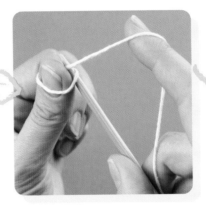

2 Take the yarn in your right hand. Wrap the yarn around the point of the needle and between your thumbs.

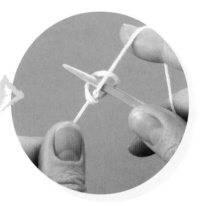

3 Draw the thread through the loop on the thumb, and then slip the loop over the edge of the needle. You have now knitted the slipknot, and are ready to make another stitch.

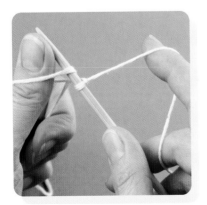

4 Repeat until you have the right amount of stitches.

TIP
Always try to knit in good light, especially when starting out. If you are bending over to look at your stitches, you will get a sore back and neck.

Between the stitch method

This is sometimes referred to as the cable or rib method. It gives a more fancy, less elastic, straight edge. To begin with, cast on two stitches using the two-needle method.

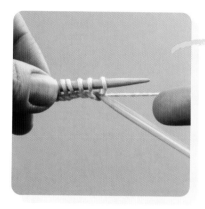

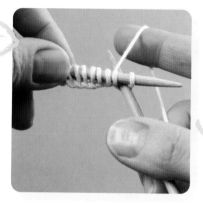

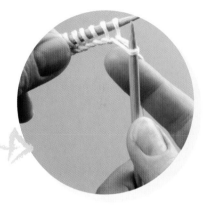

1 Place the needle between the first and second stitches.

2 Knit the loop by passing the yarn between the needles and then take the yarn through the first loop with the right needle as you've done before.

3 The new stitch will appear from between the previous stitches.

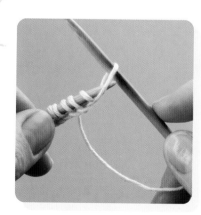

4 Put this new stitch back on the left needle with all the other stitches, and repeat until you have the right amount of stitches.

Knit stitch

Cast on the right amount of stitches for your project. When making a knit stitch the yarn is always held at the back and the right-hand needle goes through the loop from front to back.

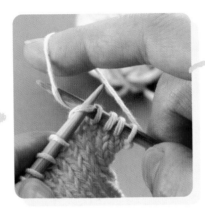

1 Insert the point of the right needle, from front to back, through the first loop on the left needle. You are forming a cross with your needles.

2 Draw the new loop through to the front of the work. Do this by pulling the left needle under the right one, pulling the new loop with it.

3 You have now made a new stitch, which is on the right-hand needle, and you need to drop the old one down to the row below. Keeping the tension with your finger, slip the old stitch off the left needle.

TIP!
When making a knit stitch the yarn is held at the back, and your right-hand needle points to the back. When making a purl stitch, your yarn is held at the front and your right-hand needle points to the front.

4 With your new stitch on the right-hand needle, repeat this whole process again until the end of the row. Turn your needles around so all the stitches are held in your left hand again. The right needle is empty and ready to take on a whole new row.

Purl stitch

Purl is done on the wrong side of the work when you are doing stockinette stitch. Obviously, it is the right side of the work if you are doing reverse stockinette stitch. It is basically a plain knit stitch in reverse, so the yarn is held in the front of the work, and this time, the needle goes from back to front.

1 Bring your yarn to the front of your work. Insert the point of the right needle from back to front, through the first loop on the left needle.

2 Pass the yarn, which is held at the front of your work, between the two points of the needles.

3 Draw the loop through to the back of the work.

✳ The apple protector is knitted in stockinette stitch, knit one row, purl the next.

4 Slip the old stitch off the left-hand needle and repeat to the end of the row.

Binding off

I always think of binding off as the full stop of knitting. It is important when acquiring a new skill to learn how to stop as well as start. A little like learning where the brakes are on your first bicycle, it is one of the most important things to learn.

Binding off, or casting off, as it is known in the UK, is a method to finish your knitting. If you don't finish it off properly it will all unravel, and you don't want that to happen.

Always bind off in the appropriate way for your work, knit-wise on a knit row, or purl-wise on a purl row. If you are casting off in rib, follow the same pattern.

1 When you are ready to bind off, knit the first two stitches of the row. With the left needle, lift the first stitch over the top of the second stitch and let it go.

2 You now are down to one stitch on your right needle. Knit one more stitch and repeat step 1. When the last stitch remains, cut the yarn and pass the tail through the last stitch.

✳ Casting off is also a term used in sailing —it means to untie a rope and sail away.

Holding the needles

When learning to knit, try lots of different ways of holding your needles. It's a bit like holding a pen, in that once you have formed the habit, it is hard to change your ways, so get it right to begin with.

These days, most of us don't need to multitask to the point of knitting with one hand, so here are some tips on holding your needles normally, with two hands. You can knit anywhere, but to start off, stay sitting down.

✳ Thumbs are really useful. Your thumbs can guide and feed the stitches up to the point of the needle. Never hold your knitting too low down. Keep your stitches near to the end of the needle and ready to be knitted!

✳ Right-hand fingers are your tension guide. The yarn comes from the ball and through your fingers ready for your index finger to wrap the yarn around the needles. Keep your index finger poised ready to stitch.

Knitting positions

1 It is best to start off with the needles held evenly in front of you, with the cross of the needles in the center.

2 The right-hand needle here is being held straight towards the body. The left-hand needle does all the moving. This way you can support the needle, and the weight of the knitting, under you arm, in a knitting sheath or stick, or in a knitting belt.

✳ *Wendy Moorby supports her needle with her right breast. Find out more about speed knitting on the next page.*

Holding the yarn

There are many different ways to hold your knitting, and the most important thing is finding a way that is comfortable for you.

I once had the pleasure of meeting Wendy Moorby, from West Yorkshire, who was the fastest knitter in the world. The end of her right-hand needle nested in her right armpit and she had her yarn wrapped so neatly around her fingers that she had very small movements, enabling her to knit faster.

Speed knitting

Wendy knitted 245 stitches in three minutes in New York in 2003. Wendy's record was beaten by Hazel Tindall from Shetland, Scotland, who won the World Speed Knitting Championships 2004, in London, with 255 stitches.

The fastest knitting speed is measured over stockinette stitch across a row of 60 stitches; using US 6 (4mm) needles and sport weight yarn. Check your speed (for three minutes) against current records—the fewer movements, the faster you get. Your fingers are sensitive and eventually you can knit without looking. It's possible to get to a stage where your thumbs can feel which stitch is coming next, and your brain will count for you while you are thinking about something else.

Old tricks

In days gone by, when knitters had to knit to keep warm, they would use a "sheath," or "stick," which enabled them to knit with one hand. These were wooden and changed shape depending on where you came from. Probably carved for you by a loved one, they were an odd phallic shape that would fit around your hip when standing or sitting, and attached to a belt so you could knit while milking the cow or walking. They are very rare to find now, so difficult to experiment with. Knitters in Shetland, Scotland, were more sensible and had a belt with a little leather cushion with holes in and double-ended needles, which slotted into the holes.

* Hold the yarn in your armpit, don't let it fall on the floor or it will get dirty...

Tensioning the yarn

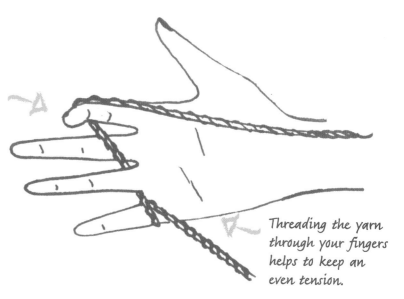

Hook the yarn over your index finger.

* If you are a knitter with a tendency to wear nail polish, choose a color to match your work, and it looks fancy when you are knitting in public.

Threading the yarn through your fingers helps to keep an even tension.

Hand positions

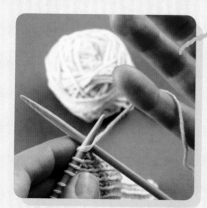

1 Hook the yarn around your little finger, palm facing up.

2 Turn the hand over and allow the yarn to flow over the ring finger and under the middle finger.

3 Finally the yarn hooks over the index finger, and it is here that the yarn is controlled.

Combinations of knit and purl

If you knit plain stitches all the time this becomes garter stitch, but if you plain knit and purl alternate rows, you have stockinette stitch. All the basic patterns and textures are based on this principle of mixing knit and purl stitches—the rough and the smooth.

Ribbing

This is the elastic stitch you find on the cuff or collar of a sweater. It is made by combining knit and purl on the same row to make vertical lines. Knit one, purl one, is the most elastic of stitches, whereas knit four, purl one will be flatter and not so stretchy. Move your yarn from front to back, between the needles when changing stitch. On the next row, knit a knit stitch on top of a knit and a purl stitch on top of a purl. If you get this the wrong way around, you will end up with another lovely stitch called seed stitch.

Simple 2 x 2 rib
(multiples of 2 stitches)
R1: knit 1, purl 1
R2: purl 1, knit 1

Seed stitch

This is knitted like ribbing, but you place a knit stitch on top of a purl stitch and vice versa. It is not elastic like ribbing, but comes out strong, flat, wider than stockinette stitch, and looks the same on both sides.

Simple seed stitch
(multiples of 2 stitches)
R1: knit1, purl 1
R2: knit 1, purl 1

Gauge and tension

Don't let worries about gauge get you in a lather. The rule is: always make a swatch. You will end up with lots of little swatched squares, but then you can use them for something useful, like a cover for your phone or MP3 player. If you sew them all together they will make a great blanket for a baby, or a cover for your favorite book (see opposite to cover this book).

To make a gauge swatch, cast on 20 stitches and knit a small square in the pattern that you will be using in your project. Flatten the swatch out, pinning it down if necessary, and then count the number of stitches and rows across a 4 inch (10cm) distance.

If the number of stitches per inch (cm) is less that the pattern gauge, try again with smaller needles. If the number is more than the pattern recommends, swap your needles for larger sized ones. Everyone has a different tension, so make sure you check yours and adjust your needles accordingly.

* You could knit a whole library...

Gauge swatches

Make gauge template out of card with a 4in hole in the center.

Count the number of rows up and down, then count the number of stitches side by side to find your gauge.

4in

4in

Sew swatches together to cover this book.

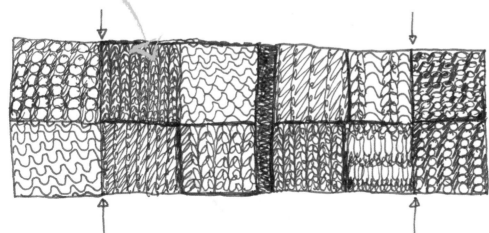

Fold at the arrows for the flaps, and sew seams together top and bottom.

Clever stuff

There are two basic stitches in knitting, knit and purl. Once you have mastered these, you can do the clever stuff—so here's how!

Elongated stitches

You can make enormous stitches to make your knitting grow faster and give a loopy, lacy effect. When wrapping the yarn between the needles, wrap it around the right-hand needle two or three times, and finish knitting the stitch as normal. Your right-hand needle will fill up with a lot of loops but you will let all these go on the next row, by knitting or purling just one stitch as normal.

Making elongated stitches

Wrap the yarn around the needle twice.

On the next row, purl only one loop and let the rest drop down.

Making holes

Making holes is the basis of all lace knitting. There are many ways to make holes—and you will discover most of them when you are learning to knit. To make a hole properly, in a controlled way, try these steps on the right.

You lose one stitch by knitting two together, but you gain one stitch when the yarn goes back around to the back. You can do this purl-wise, by taking your yarn to the back, and then purling two stitches together. It's the same principle, just the other way around.

1 To make a hole knit-wise, wrap the yarn around the right needle, before you make a stitch.

2 Then knit two stitches together and continue to the end of the row. On the next row, knit the yarn over as a stitch—et voilá, a hole.

Making cables

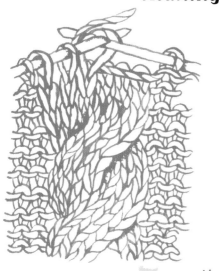

Make a right twist...
or a left one.

*Golly all this
knitting is making
me sleepy...*

Cable stitches

Cabling is when you take your stitches off in different directions or twist them around each other. Fishermen have it on their sweaters, I guess because it looks like twisted rope. There are many patterns to be made by doing this. You need a cable needle. If you want to move the next stitches to the left, put them on the cable needle and hold them at the front of the work. Knit the next stitches and then the stitches from the cable needle.

To move stitches to the right, slip the stitches onto the cable needle, and hold at the back of the work. Knit the next stitches that are moving right and then knit the stitches from the cable needle.

Make a bobble

To make bobbles on your knitting, increase a few extra stitches in one stitch and knit or purl backwards and forwards for a few rows on these new stitches until a bobble grows out of your work. Once the bobble is the right size, bind off the extra stitches by passing them over the first stitch and carry on across your row as normal. You can push your bobble to the front or the back of your work, and make the bobble in whatever stitch you like.

Making ladders

Just drop a stitch on purpose and run it all the way to the bottom of your knitting. Ooh, that feels good!

Increasing

To make your knitting wider or narrower, you need to learn to increase and decrease stitches. Once you have learned this you can knit almost anything, including things like cardigans, bras, and cakes.

There are lots of ways to increase, but the simplest is the lifted strand increase. Work to the place where the increase is required, and insert the tip of the right-hand needle under the horizontal loop between the stitches, from front to back. Now insert the tip of the left needle from front to back through the loop and take it onto the left needle. Insert the tip of the right needle through the back of the new stitch.

This twists the stitch. Knit the twisted stitch normally. When increasing this way on a purl row, twist the stitch by inserting the right needle from back to front into the back of the loop.

Knitting between the stitches can cause a slight hole, so alternatively, you can knit into the back of a stitch, as shown here. Knit the first stitch, but instead of dropping it off the left needle, knit into the back of it again.

Fully fashioned increasing

1 Knit two stitches at the start of the row. Knit the following stitch, and then knit into the back of that stitch as well.

If you knit into the back of the stitch two or three stitches away from the edge of the row, or even in the middle of a row, it will make a neat line called a fashioning mark.

This is the most professional way to increase and actually makes it easier to keep a track of how many stitches you have increased. If you count the marks you will know how many extra stitches you have made. Visible shaping is used as a design feature. You may have wondered what those marks were in machine made knitting, so now you know.

Decreasing

This is a crucial part of shaping your knitting. Simply knit or purl two stitches together. You can decrease anywhere in a row. If you do it at the beginning of a row it may make a bobbly edge. Fully fashioned shaping avoids this, while also creating an attractive pattern in your fabric.

Decreasing on the edge

1 Knitting two together at the beginning of the row is simple, but can make a bobbly edge.

2 A fully-fashioned decrease can make a neat edge. Knit two or more single stitches at the beginning of a row, then knit two together.

* *You can see the shaping marks on the sections here.*

Joining a new ball of yarn

If your yarn runs out, or you wish to change color, you just need to tie a knot. Do this at the beginning of a row. Leave 6 inches (15cm) on the end of your original yarn. Tie a square or reef knot with the new yarn, again leaving about 6 inches (15cm). Make sure the knot is neatly pushed right up to the next stitch. Knots always come undone in the end, so when you have finished your knitting you can untie this knot and sew in the ends. Warning! Don't find yourself knitting with the loose ends by mistake—that can just be plain annoying.

Loose ends

Knitters are rarely at a loose end because there is always knitting to do. We have loose ends in our work though and here's how to fix them.

✻ An iron is always useful.

Pressing

Ironing does wonders for your knitting. Place pieces wrong side up on an ironing board or a board. Pin your work out, with all the rows in straight lines, and no stretching. Check the ironing instructions for the type of yarn used. For flat fabrics, place a clean, damp dish towel over the top and put the iron on a warm setting. For fluffy or textured fabrics put your iron on the big steam setting and hover the iron just above the surface. Steam away!

Synthetic fibers might not take to ironing, so pin these out as normal. Spray with water to dampen the fabric, and then leave to dry naturally. The knitting will instantly look much more professional.

Weaving in the ends

Loose ends are left when you change color or add on a new ball of yarn. It helps if you leave the ends about 6 inches (15cm) long. This is long enough to thread through a tapestry or darning needle and weave into the back of the knitting or along a seam.

Undo the knot that was made when you joined the yarns together. Thread the needle with one of the tails of yarn. On the back of your knitting, weave in and out of stitches the same color horizontally for about six stitches, or along the edge of your knitting vertically. Now take the needle back through the woven-in stitches to catch them. Stretch the knitting to make sure the loose ends are secure, and then cut off the loose end. Repeat for the other threads.

Linking together

Great knitters of days gone by didn't always use sewing to construct their clothes. Seams were sometimes knitted together, making them much stronger, and avoiding cases of sleeves blowing off in severe weather conditions.

Sewing is quite adequate these days, and there are a few stitches you can use. It is advisable to use the same yarn that you knitted with, unless you want the stitches to be a feature of your work.

✻ Finishing your work properly is important.

Mattress stitch

Mattress stitch is a neat stitch, which can hardly be seen from the right side.

Grafting is neat but tricky...

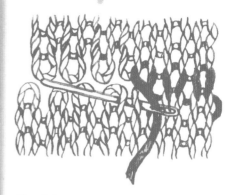

1 Lay the pieces to be joined together right side up. Leaving the end of the yarn at the back of the work to sew in later, bring the needle through to the front, in the middle of the first stitch one row from the edge. Take the needle through to the same position on the other piece, and bring it out in the middle of the next stitch one row up.

2 Insert the needle back into the first piece of fabric, in the same place that the yarn last came out. Then bring the needle out in the middle of the stitch above. Repeat this making a zig-zag seam from edge to edge for a few more rows. You can pull the thread tight and the stitches almost disappear. When the seam is finished, sew in the loose ends.

Grafting

This is another flat seam that doesn't require you to bind off. Lay the edges together on a flat surface and match them stitch for stitch. Run your needle and thread through each stitch, making shapes that emulate the stitches of the fabric. If you use the same yarn that you knitted with, the seam should be invisible.

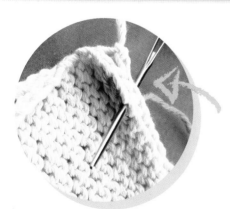

Backstitch

This is a really useful stitch that is quickly learned. Place the pieces to be joined with the right sides facing each other. Make small stitches—two steps forward, and one step back—to create a secure seam.

TIP

If you are in a rush to finish a garment for Saturday night and you don't have time to stitch it together, just use safety pins, or stick it straight onto your body with hypoallergenic sticky tape.

Disasters

Don't panic! Disasters can usually be fixed with a bit of patience. Sometimes disasters can become features, with a bit of imagination. Here are a few tips on how to cope.

Dropping stitches

Move slowly, and place your knitting, knit side up, on a convenient surface. Switch a bright light on, assess the situation, and grab a crochet hook or smaller needle.

Above your dropped stitch, you will notice horizontal threads. These are the threads from the above rows. By counting these you can tell how many rows the stitch has fallen down.

If you are picking up a knit stitch, place the loose stitch on top of the next horizontal thread and, using the crochet hook, pull the horizontal thread through the stitch. Repeat this up the rows. To pick up a purl stitch, the horizontal thread is on top of the stitch and you pull it through from behind. Place the stitch back on the left-hand needle and carry on as normal.

Unraveling your knitting

You may need to unravel your knitting if you have been daydreaming and knitted too far. To do this, place it down on a table, take your needle out, and gently pull the thread back to the desired length, one row at a time. Slide your needle back through the stitches. If it's a fancy yarn and this is difficult, slide a smaller needle in to begin with and then transfer them back to the right size needle.

✳ Unravel your knitting one row at a time...

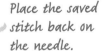

Picking up a dropped stitch

First, assess the damage...

Then, pick up the stitch with a hook or needle.

To pick up a purl stitch, bring the hook behind the ladder.

Place the saved stitch back on the needle.

Recycling yarn

Sometimes we grow out of our knitwear, and it's loved so much that the only thing to do is unravel it and save as much yarn as you can before it goes in the trash. My friend Arthur knitted a gray scarf out of some gray yarn that was once my dad's sweater and smelled of wood from when he was chopping logs. It gives the finished product a special story.

Here is how you do it...

The garment shouldn't be too damaged. It won't work if it has felted in the washing machine. If the garment is dirty, you can wash the yarn once it is unraveled.

Shake the garment to remove any dust, and then un-pick the seams, taking out any bits of sewing yarn. Taking each piece, find the last stitch of the bound off edge. Pull it out and proceed to unpick the knitting, but be careful not to pull the yarn too hard. If the stitches catch, be gentle, they will come apart if you persevere. Wind the yarn into a ball. You will notice that as you unravel, the yarn will appear wavy.

The next step is to make the yarn up into skeins. Drop the ball into a pot or jam jar. Now wind the yarn into a skein either on a skein holder or between your thumb and fingers and your elbow. The skein must be tied in several places to keep it in shape and to prevent the yarn getting tangled. Now you are ready to either wash or steam the yarn. This will make it straight again, and as good as new.

When it is first unraveled, the yarn will be wavy like this.

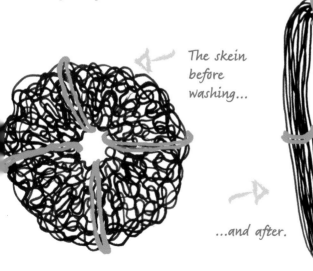

The skein before washing...

...and after.

If you don't keep your yarn tidy, it will end up looking like this.

The mending pile

We've all had knitwear that is impossible to part with. Holes are tragic, but they can be fixed with good old-fashioned darning.

Holes in knitted garments happen for many different reasons. You do not have to throw holey clothes away. Darning is a neat way for fixing holes and it gives garments a whole new life and character.

Knitting garments you really love and bond with means they are likely to be worn for years and years and will eventually start to form holes. Elbows wear thin on sweaters, and toes start poking through socks.

To avoid elbows wearing through, you can cut oval-shaped patches of leather and sew them on in the position of the elbows. To make socks last longer, the heels and toes can be knitted with double thread.

✳ Mending can be creative, rather than a struggle…

Beware the dreaded moth!

Take care when packing your woollies away. Moths can creep into your wardrobe when you are not looking and munch their way through the middle of your favorite woolens. Mothballs smell bad, but they do keep your clothes safe. Wrap your sweaters in paper bags if you're really worried. There are old-fashioned remedies for this perennial problem including lavender bags, cedarwood, and oil, and my favorite one, horse chestnuts steeped in cedar oil.

When I was younger, a mouse ate through a sweater I had knitted. I think it wanted some fluff for its nest. Mice make much bigger holes than moths, and I can only suggest knitting a patch to cover the hole.

A stitch in time saves nine

Darning can be hidden or it can be decorative. Hidden darning is easier if you have the same yarn. Try to keep a small amount of leftover yarn in your wool stash whenever you finish a garment. You might be glad of it ten years later.

Darning

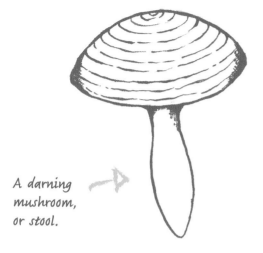

A darning mushroom, or stool.

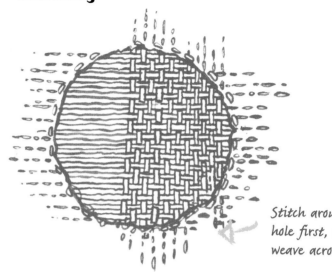

Stitch around the hole first, then weave across.

How to darn

You need a darning mushroom, a darning needle, and thread. Find some yarn to darn with. It helps if the yarn is slightly thinner than the yarn used for knitting the garment. If you are using the same yarn as the garment, try removing a strand from the ply. However, a darning needle should have a good-sized eye to pass yarn through.

Darning mushrooms are usually wooden and are hard to find these days. If you don't have one, you can use a tennis ball instead. Darning mushrooms are used to ensure a flat darn on a large hole. The curved head of the mushroom sits under the hole and you hold the stalk of the mushroom with your left hand to hold the hole in place. The principle of darning over a hole is similar to weaving, where you have threads going from top to bottom across the hole, and then you weave threads in from side to side across the hole. On the outskirts of the hole, the stitching needs to blend into the fabric about four to five stitches in from the edge. If part of the garment is wearing thin, and looks like a hole could be coming, then you can strengthen it by running stitches vertically along the stockinette stitches.

Darning is less noticeable if done from the wrong side, but if the hole is to be close to your skin, like the heel of a sock, it will be more comfortable if done on the right side.

Getting rid of pilling

Over time little fluff balls can develop under the arms of sweaters and around the heels of socks. This is where the fluff on the surface of the sweater has rubbed together into a ball, and stuck to the fabric under another layer of fluff. They can make a sweater look tired and old, but they are easy to remove. Either brush or comb the sweater, or attack it with sticky tape by putting the sticky side down and ripping it off. The sticky tape trick is good all over the garment, as it lifts the pile and makes it look good as new. A light iron also helps.

Washing day

After all that loving work, our knitwear must stay fresh, so we roll up our sleeves for laundry day.

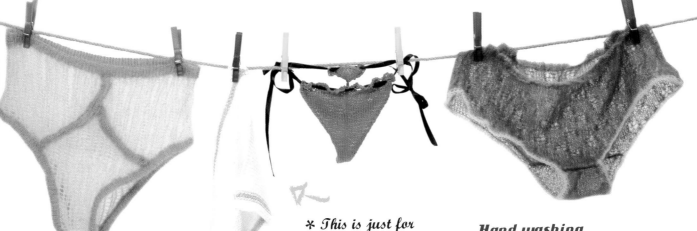

✷ This is just for show! Knitting should really be dried flat.

Washing your knitting

Knitted items change in the washing process. This can be good or bad, depending on what you are trying to do. It is a wise idea to keep the labels from the yarn that you are using so that you will know how to treat it when the time comes.

Felting

As it is thrown around in the washing machine or tumble dryer, the little fibers within the yarn curl and cling to each other, tighter and tighter, and felting occurs. This can be a disaster, but it is also a process you can use to make interesting effects, or to make your garment smaller if you knitted it too big.

Felt can be ironed with a coolish iron while it is still wet. Felt is very tough, but there is also some flexibility to change shape while it's wet. You can pull it out and pin it to a board, so it can dry in the way you want.

Hand washing

To wash a woolen or silk fabric in a normal way, wash by hand in cool or luke warm water with some soft soap made for wool. Don't be too rough, just swill it around a bit and hum some tunes until the water has become dirty. Drain off the dirty water and rinse with clean water. Keep doing this until all the soap has gone. To dry, squeeze as much of the water out as you can but don't wring it. Lay out your knitting on an old towel, pulling it into the shape that you want.

Cotton or linen knitwear can be washed in hot water, but not so hot that you burn your hands! Synthetic knitwear can sometimes be put in the washing machine, but otherwise wash by hand at 90°F (40°C).

Dry with care

Hanging a knitted garment up to dry makes its shape change. This is not always what you want, but you can get some interesting effects. Hanging things up on a washing line with clothes pegs will make things grow longer and longer as the water drains out. If you want to make sleeves really long, attach little weights and hang them up.

Try to avoid hanging a knitted sweater on a door handle or the back of a chair. It tends to make a bulge come out of the back of your neck or causes strange lumps appear in your shoulder area, which isn't a good look.

Care label lingo

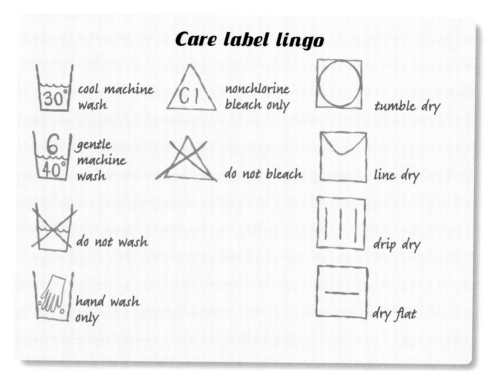

- 30° cool machine wash
- 6 40° gentle machine wash
- do not wash
- hand wash only
- C1 nonchlorine bleach only
- do not bleach
- tumble dry
- line dry
- drip dry
- dry flat

Ironing and drycleaning

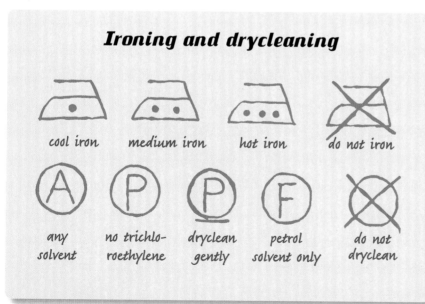

- cool iron
- medium iron
- hot iron
- do not iron
- A any solvent
- P no trichloroethylene
- P dryclean gently
- F petrol solvent only
- do not dryclean

✻ Cool water is best for washing wool. Dry cleaning is smelly, but it does keep the moths away.

a cake that is calorie free...

thoroughly modern Harriet wears bows

all good things come to those who wait...

Domestic Bliss

how do you like your eggs, fried or crocheted?

would you care for a sandwich?

My first dishcloth

Put a bit of love into doing the dishes! A hand-knitted dishcloth is less likely to be left in a rotting heap on the draining board. Knitted in pure cotton, it can be washed and bleached time and time again. Experiment with different stitches and edgings, and feel proud as you leave it draped and drying over the taps. Ideal as a novice knitting project, or for those keen on handicraft hygiene.

You will need...

MEASUREMENTS:
Approx 11.5 x 9.5in (29 x 24cm)

YARN: Pure cotton yarn in sport weight
1 x 1oz (25g) ball in color A, oddment
in color B

NEEDLES: US 6 (4mm)

GAUGE: 20 sts/38 rows = 4in (10cm)
in garter st. The tension is not critical
in this pattern, provided a change in
size is acceptable

✱ Find the key
to the abbreviations
on page 137.

Directions

Using A, cast on 58 sts and work 6 rows g-st (knit each row).

Using B, knit 4 rows.

Using A knit until cloth measures 8–12in (20–30cm) from beg.

Using B, knit 4 rows.

Using A, knit 6 rows and bind off.

Making up:

Sew in ends securely and you are ready to wash.

Bows for furnishing and fashion

An accessory you didn't realize you needed until you started knitting them, knitted bows can be used to decorate your clothing or for interior décor. In the home, use your bows to hide unsightly picture hooks or holes in the upholstery. Shown here in sport weight yarn on US 6 (4mm) needles but try knitting them with other yarn and needle sizes as well. Make some bows in Lurex for Christmas tree decorations and they are great for gift wrapping too, but start early or you'll still be knitting away on Christmas Eve.

You will need...

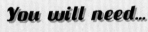

MEASUREMENTS: Bow width 6½ x 7½in (19 x 16.5cm) to tip of "tails"

YARN: Sport weight approx 1 x 1oz (25g) ball

NEEDLES: US 6 (4mm)

GAUGE: Not required

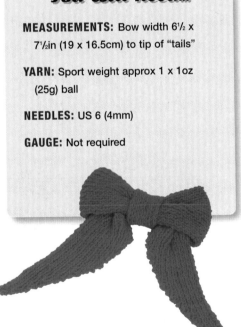

Directions

Loops:
Work 2 alike.
Cast on 22 sts and work in k1, p1 rib for 5.5in (14cm).
Bind off.

Tails:
Work 2 alike.
Cast on 2 sts. Working in k1, p1 rib, m1 st at beg of 2nd and every foll alt row until 22 sts. Work straight in rib until tail measures 5.5in (14cm) and bind off.

Middle strap:
Cast on 16 sts and work in k1, p1 rib until strap measures 2.5in (6.5cm).
Bind off.

Making up:
Fold the pieces for the loops in half and pleat, sew securely.
Pleat the straight ends of the pointed pieces and sew into the loops. Wrap the small strip to form the knot, stitch into place, and the bow is complete.

More bows...

* Attach a bow to a strong hair clip for windy high seas.

Brighten up a lampshade!

✳ *Highlight your best features with a well-placed decorative accessory.*

✳ *Put your best foot forward with a shiny pink bow to decorate your knickerbockers.*

Apple protector

This knitted fruit cover is perfect to save your snack from the indignity of being bumped around in your backpack whether you are on the train to work, hiking up a mountain, or just having a relaxing picnic.

You will need...

MEASUREMENTS:
Will stretch to fit most apples

YARN: Sport weight cotton 1 x 1oz (25g) ball in red, oddment in green

NEEDLES: US 6 (4mm)   **GAUGE:** Not required

Directions

Apple sections:

Work 3 alike. Cast on 2 sts in red. Starting with a knit row, work in st st throughout. Inc 1 st at beg of each row until 14 sts. Work 2 rows straight. Dec 1 st at beg of next 10 rows.

Next row: K2tog twice*.

Bind off.

For the open section, work as given for other apple sections to *. Cast on 8 sts. Bind off all sts.

Leaf:

Using green, cast on 3 sts.

Row 1: K1, m1, k1, m1, k1. 5 sts.

Row 2: This row and every other row, purl.

Row 3: K1, m1, k3, m1, k1. 7 sts.

Row 4: Purl one row then work 2 rows straight.

Row 7: K1, k2tog, k1, k2tog, k1. 5 sts.

Row 9: K1, sl1, k2tog psso, k1. 3 sts.

Row 10 : p1 p2tog. 2 sts.

Bind off rem sts.

Bobble button:

Cast on 2 sts in red.

Row 1: Knit, inc in each st, 4 sts.

Work 5 rows st st (starting with purl row).

Next row: K2tog twice.

Bind off.

Sew the sections together at the sides

Making up: Join apple sections leaving just one seam open (between plain section and the one with the cast on/ bind off bit on it) at point where they reach maximum width. Roll up bobble button and slip stitch it to form a firm bobble then sew it to top of adjacent open section. Sew leaf start to top edge so that when it folds back right side is visible. Complete loop by slip stitching down loose end of cast on, bind off bit. Insert apple to shape!

Fried-egg earmuffs

Hate the sound of eggs frying? Survive in style with these super fried-egg earmuffs. Inspired by the eponymous hangover cure, these eggs will help keep the volume down. Held in place by a simple chained loop they are easy to crochet, even if you have never handled a hook before.

You will need...

MEASUREMENTS:
One size fits all!

YARN: Fingering weight mercerized cotton 1 x 1oz (25g) balls in each of white (A) and yellow (B)

NEEDLES: US D (3mm) crochet hook

GAUGE: Not required

✻ These eggs are sunny-side up, but you can make yours over easy if you prefer.

Directions

Egg white: Work 2 alike.

Using A, wrap yarn around in a circle and then work 7 sc into circle, join with a sl st to first sc.

Row 2: 1 ch (as first sc) 1 sc in same place as sl st, *2 sc in next sc, rep from * to end. Sl st in first ch.

Row 3: As row 2.

Row 4: 1 ch (as first sc), *1 sc in next sc, 2 sc in next sc, rep from * ending sl st in first ch.

Row 5: 1 ch (as first sc), *miss 1 sc, 1 sc in next sc, rep from * to end with sl st in first sc.

Yolk: Work 2 alike.

Using B, wrap yarn around in a circle and then work 5 sc into circle, join with a sl st to first sc.

Row 2: 1 ch (as first sc) 1 sc in same place as sl st, *2 sc in next sc, rep from * to end. Sl st in first ch.

Row 3: 1 ch (as first sc), *1 sc in next sc, 2 sc in next sc, rep from * ending sl st in first ch and fasten off.

Row 4: 1 ch, *dec 1 st over next 2 sc thus: (hook through next sc, pull lp through) twice, yoh, pull through all lps on hook, dec over next 3 sc thus: (hook through next sc, pull lp through) 3 times, yoh, pull through all lps on hook, rep from * once more, dec over last 3 sc, sl st to first sc and fasten off.

Ear chain: Work 2 alike.

Join A to a st on last row of egg white. Work approx 6-8 ch (long enough to hook over your ear to keep earmuff on), join to opposite side of white with a slip stitch and fasten off.

Making up: Slip stitch yoke centrally to white, or off-center, as shown.

Variation: Try fried green tomatoes.

Making a circle

1. Wind yarn around in a loop and insert hook into loop front to back (yarn at left is from ball).

2. Pull loop through, wrap yarn around hook, and then put hook through loop again.

3. Pull loop on hook through to fasten off the stitch.

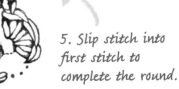

4. Work sc (UK dc) into wound loop.

5. Slip stitch into first stitch to complete the round.

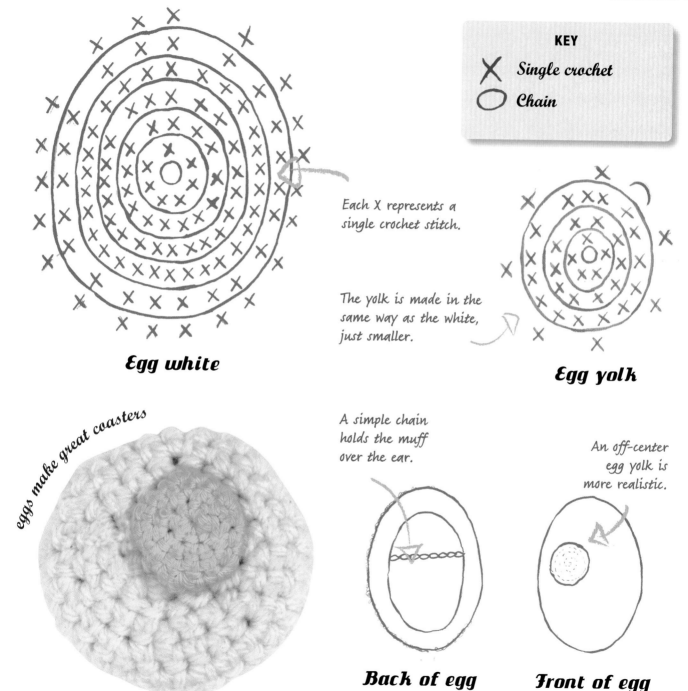

KEY

✗ Single crochet

◯ Chain

Egg white

Each X represents a single crochet stitch.

The yolk is made in the same way as the white, just smaller.

Egg yolk

eggs make great coasters

A simple chain holds the muff over the ear.

An off-center egg yolk is more realistic.

Back of egg

Front of egg

Shoelaces

Spool knitting is a great way to make cords. Use as many strands together as you like. Buy yourself a spool knitting bobbin or make your own with a sewing thread spool and four nails. Experiment with using several thinner threads at one time. Lurex is a good strong metallic thread and should be tough for regular daily use. Make firm tips, or aglets, with adhesive tape and a dab of glue, or attach pom-poms.

You will need...

MEASUREMENTS:
Lengths will vary from 27 to 72in (69 to 180 cm)

YARN: Pink Lurex

EQUIPMENT: Spool knitting bobbin

GAUGE: Not crucial

Spool knitting

Wind the yarn around the first pin clockwise.

This is what it looks like from the top.

Directions

To begin, pass your yarn all the way through the bobbin, from head to toe. To cast on, wrap the yarn around the first pin, or make a slipknot. Moving clockwise from one pin to another, wrap the yarn around the pin twice in a counterclockwise direction. Using a sharp pointed stick or knitting needle, pick up the lower stitch and pass it over the top of the pin.

Start here.

Spool knitting

On the following rounds, wrap the yarn around all four pins, then hook over the loop underneath.

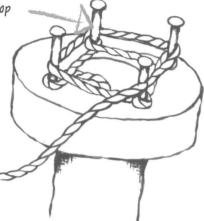

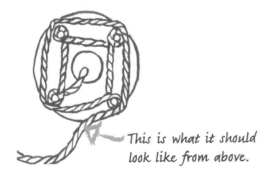

This is what it should look like from above.

For the following rows you need only wrap the pin once, passing the existing stitch over the new wrap. Keep going around in the same direction. As you complete more rows cord will start to appear at the bottom of your bobbin. Continue until you reach the desire length. Bind off, thread the yarn in a large needle, and pick up each stitch, pulling them off the pins, and draw it tight. The resulting cord can then be coiled and stitched to create a decorative brooch.

Making up:
Attach adhesive tape to secure the ends and cut off any extra yarn. For extra security, place a dab of clear adhesive or superglue on the ends before attaching the tape. Roll the ends between your fingers, so that the knitted cord is compressed, and then fold the tape around it, cutting off any excess with sharp scissors.

Lacing:
Shoelaces can be as long or as short as you need for your particular style of shoes, sneakers, hiking boots, and so on.

It is important to get the right length of shoelace, otherwise you could be tripping over on the sidewalk, which is not clever. How long you need your laces to be, depends on the lacing method you prefer, the number of eyelets, or holes, and how far away they are from each other. You also need to allow extra for the bow, and here you are into personal preference territory. Some like a small neat bow, others like extra for tying double knots and other fancy stuff. Alternatively, lay your old laces out straight, and make your new ones the exact same length.

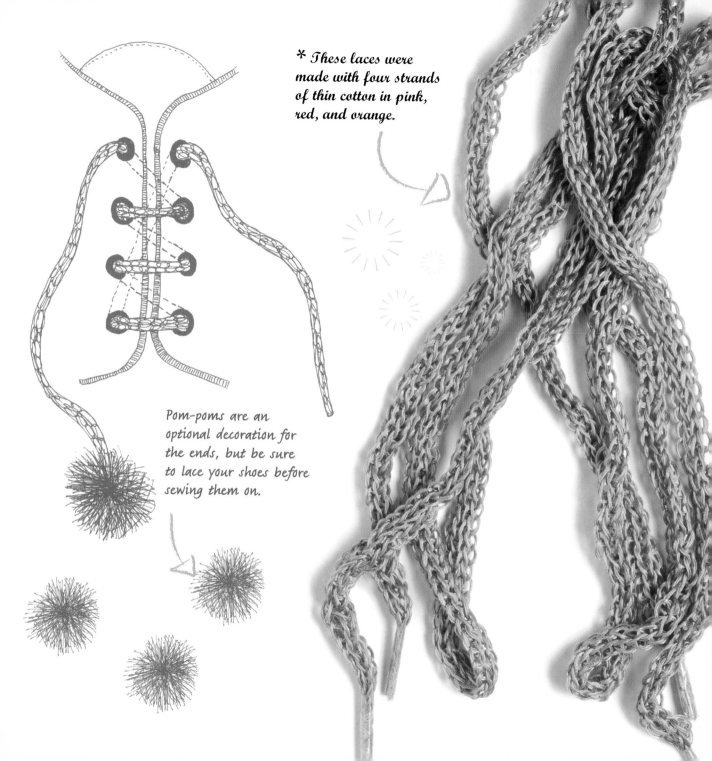

* These laces were made with four strands of thin cotton in pink, red, and orange.

Pom-poms are an optional decoration for the ends, but be sure to lace your shoes before sewing them on.

Duster glove

Greet your neighbors with this unique cleaning glove. Buffing has never been so much fun. Mark's cleaning a window here, but in his spare time he collects knickknacks, so I made him a glove to dust them. You could wear them when you go out and then you can dust and buff anywhere!

The palms are made in fur stitch and the other side is white. Knit in sport weight cotton for softness, or acrylic if you like to create static when dusting.

You will need...

MEASUREMENTS:
To fit a medium/large hand

YARN: Sport weight cotton or acrylic,
1 x 1oz ball (25g) in each of white (A)
and yellow (B)

NEEDLES: US 6 (4mm)

GAUGE: Not required

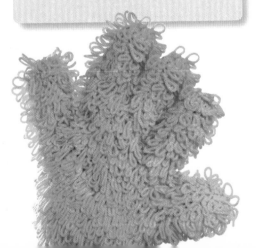

Special notes

Fur stitch is worked thus:

Row 1: K1 (as selvage), *k next st but do not let st slip off the needle. Bring yf between the needles and take it under the left thumb from back to front making a loop of desired length (see diagram over page). Knit into the same st again and slip original st off the LH needle keeping thumb in the loop. With thumb still in loop, insert LH needle through the front of the 2 sts just made and k2tog through the back. Slip thumb out of loop. Rep from * to last st, k1.

Row 2: Purl.

These 2 rows form fur fabric and are rep throughout.

Directions

Smooth side: Work 1.

Using A, cast on 48 sts and work in k1, p1 rib for 15 rows.

Next Row: K6, m1, k12, m1, k6, slip next 24 sts onto a stitch holder and cont on first 26 sts.

Cont in st st and work 3 rows.

*Increase Row:** K1, m1 st, k to end.

Work 3 rows st st. Rep from * until 6 inc have been worked (32 sts) ending with a purl row.

Smooth side continued:

Shape thumb: K10 sts, turn. Cont on these sts only for thumb and work a further 19 rows straight.

Next Row: K1, k2tog 4 times, k1. 6 sts.

Next Row: Purl.

Next Row: K2tog 3 times, 3 sts.

Next Row: P3tog and fasten off.

Shape hand:

RS facing return to rem 24 sts. Work in st st for 15 rows ending with purl row.

Shape little finger: Knit across 6 sts and turn.

Cont on these 6 sts for little finger and work straight in st st for 14 rows.

**Next Row: K1, k2tog 2 times, k1. 3 sts.

Next Row: P3tog and fasten off.

Shape next finger: Knit across 6 sts and turn. Cont on these 6 sts for next finger and work straight in st st for 16 rows. Complete as for little finger from ** to end.

Shape middle finger: Knit across 6 sts and turn. Cont on these 6 sts for next finger and work straight in st st for 18 rows. Complete as for little finger from ** to end.

Shape first finger: Knit across 6 sts and turn. Cont on these 6 sts for next finger and work straight in st st for 16 rows. Complete as for little finger from ** to end.

Fur palm:

RS facing, using B, pick up sts from stitch holder and k6, m1, k12, m1, k6.

Start and work in fur stitch (see notes on p.62) throughout and, at the same time, shape glove as given for first part, reversing shapings (work them on purl rows).

✻ *It's easy to shake out the dust while the duster is on your hand.*

Making up:

Sew glove hand and finger seams—you will find that fur section is a little bigger than plain section, just allow this side to overlap smooth side slightly.

Fur stitch

Loop the yarn around your fingers.

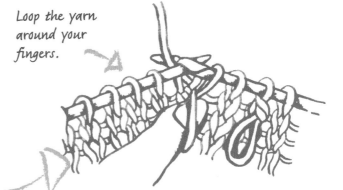

* The longer length of the yarn here will help to trap all that dirt.

High tea (very British)

Why not sit around a kitchen table having a good chat and knit your tea. Annie and the folks from Flat B have been doing that and here is their selection. If someone comes around who is not a confident knitter, ask them to knit lettuce or cheese for the sandwiches. More experienced knitters can invent fancy frosting.

Jelly roll
Directions

Cake: Using A cast on 22 sts. Work in st st (knit 1 row, purl 1 row) until piece measures 6.5in (16.5cm) and bind off.

Frosting: Using B cast on 20 sts and work as for cake until piece measures 6in (15cm) and bind off.

Making up:

Roll up white piece, and sew brown piece around it. Use chain stitch and red to embroider jelly at each end as shown.

✳ Fluffy red mohair creates the most realistic jelly to seep out of the ends of this knitted jelly roll.

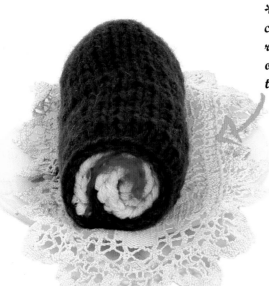

You will need...

MEASUREMENTS:
Jelly roll approx 6½in (16.5cm) long

YARN:
Jelly roll: Bulky mohair (chunky)
1 x 1oz (25g) ball in brown (A),
oddments in each of white (B)
and red (C)
Battenberg cake: Sport weight
chenille in lemon (D), pink (E),
and white (F)
Bakewell tart: Fingering wool in
beige (G) and cotton in white (H)
and red (J)

NEEDLES:
Jelly roll and Battenberg cake:
US 6 (4mm)
Bakewell tart: US 4 (3.5mm) and
US E (3mm) crochet hook

GAUGE: Not required

Battenberg cake
Directions

Using F, cast on 14 sts and knit 2 rows. Start and work in st
st (knit 1 row, purl 1 row) and work 4 rows. Knit 2 rows.
*Using D work 2 rows st st. Continue in st st and using E,
work 5 sts, D work 5 sts, E work 5 sts. Rep last row 3 times
(4 rows in all).

Change checks:

Continue in st st and using D work 5 sts, E work 5 sts, D
work 5 sts. Rep last row 3 times (4 rows in all). Using D
work 2 rows st st*.

Using F knit 2 rows. Work 4 rows in st st. Knit 2 rows. Rep
from * to * once more and bind off.

Cake sides:

Work 2 alike.

Using F, cast on 10 sts and knit 2 rows. Start and work in st
st (knit 1 row, purl 1 row) and work 4 rows. Knit 2 rows and
bind off.

Making up:

Sew white cast on edge to colored bound off edge. Stuff
cake to a square shape. Sew on the remaining two sides.

* Using chenille
gives the cake a
spongy-look texture.

Battenberg cake chart

□ D
▨ E
□ F
⊡ Reverse st st

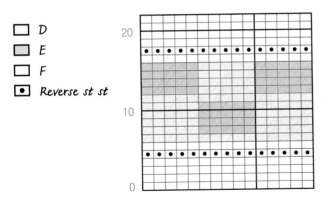

Bakewell tarts
(very British)
Directions

Pastry: Using G, cast on 32 sts and work 8 rows k1, p1 rib. Starting with a knit row work 6 rows st st.

Next Row: *K2tog, yo, rep from * to end.

Next Row: Purl.

Work 2 rows st st and bind off.

Frosting: Using H make a yarn circle (as for fried-egg earmuffs—see page 56) and using a crochet hook work 6 dc into it.

Row 2: 1 ch (as first dc), 1 dc in same place as ch, 2 dc in each dc.

Row 3: 1 ch (as first dc), *2 dc in next dc, 1 dc in next dc, rep from * to end.

Row 4: 1 ch (as first dc), *1 dc in next dc, 2 dc in next dc, rep from * to end.

Rep rows 3 and 4 two more times.

Next Row: 1 dc in each dc, fasten off.

Cherry: Using J make a yarn circle and using crochet hook, work 4 dc into it.

Next 2 rows: 1 dc in each dc—continuing in same direction (i.e. do not turn).

Next Row: *1 dc in next dc, 2 dc in next dc, rep from * once more.

Next 2 rows: 1 dc in each dc—continuing in same direction (i.e. do not turn). Fasten off leaving approx 6in (15cm) end. Thread end through last row and pull up tightly to form cherry shape, threading end through to base of cherry (this can be used to sew cherry onto the cake).

Making up:

Fold over at eyelet row and slip stitch down to form pastry lip. Join pastry seam. Sew frosting circle to bound off edge of st st pastry. Thread cast on end through bottom of pastry, stuff cake, and pull up thread at base to form shape. Secure neatly. Sew on red crochet button to top center of frosting.

Crimping the pastry

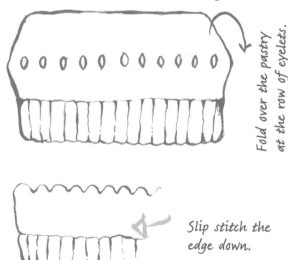

Fold over the pastry at the row of eyelets.

Slip stitch the edge down.

Chocolate cake (international yum)

Of course, a good chocolate cake can make or break your coffee mornings. The cake must be beautifully presented, luscious, and tempting, while also being completely calorie free. Forget Sara Lee and Mrs. Fields, just knit your own. We show you how.

You will need...

YARN: Sport weight 1 x 1oz (25g) ball in brown (A). Fingering mohair 1 x 1oz (25g) ball in white (B) and oddment of chenille

NEEDLES: US 6 (4mm) and crochet hook size E (3.5mm)

MATERIALS: Card for backing

GAUGE: 20 sts/38 rows = 4in (10cm) in garter st

Directions

Top of cake:

Using A cast on 15 sts. *Knit to last st, turn, and purl back. Knit to last 2 sts, turn, and purl back. Knit to last 3 sts, turn, and purl back. Keep working in this way, leaving 1 extra st at the end of each knit row until there are no more sts to leave. Knit across all the sts and purl back. Rep from * 3 more times (4 sections in all) and bind off.

(You need 5 sections to make a circle but someone has already eaten one piece of cake—hence we only have 4 sections!)

Cake sides:

Measure the circumference of the cake (see diagram over page) to determine the length, and work out how tall you want your cake. Using A, cast on and start to work in st st (knit 1 row, purl 1 row) throughout. Work until long enough to cover the cake sides, including the sides of the missing section.

❋ Someone has already eaten a slice of this tasty cake...

Making up the cake

Ease the cake around the circle of card with running stitch.

Loose stitches across the base hold the cake together.

Making up:

Pin the cake top out to a circle shape and press gently. From the card, cut out a circle which is ½in (1cm) smaller than the cake. Thread yarn through the edge of your cake leaving the end of thread long enough to pull for gathering. Cover the card with the cake, pulling the yarn end to gather the edge. Sew cake sides to cake. Make a rectangle out of card the same length as the diameter of your cake (B). Ease the cake over the top and fit by sewing long stitches across the base. Sew crocheted frosting in position on top of cake.

✱ We used mohair for the top frosting and chenille for the layers.

Frosting on the cake:

Row 1: Using B and crochet hook, work chains as long as you need for "A."

Row 2: 6 ch, slip these into 4th st from last ch made in last row, rep to end.

6 ch, slip these into the middle of the arch worked in last row, rep this procedure until the frosting is big enough to cover the cake.

Frosting for the layers:

Using B and the crochet hook, work chains long enough to reach all around the cake "B" including the sides of the extra slice "C."

Frosting on the cake

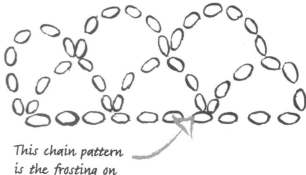

This chain pattern is the frosting on the cake.

Frosting for the layers

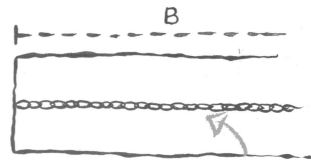

B

Measure the diameter (B) to make the sides.

Crochet a chain to fit around the outside— this is the creamy layer inside.

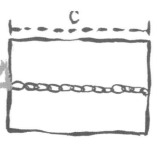

C

Crochet an extra section of frosting for the slices.

Ham sandwich

The sandwich bread and ham are in stockinette stitch and the lettuce and cheese in any stitch you like. The fillings can be in any weight of yarn but I suggest the bread should be in bread-colored sport weight.

You will need...

YARN: Sport weight 1 x 1oz (25g) ball in colors for bread (off-white or brown), ham (pale pink), cheese (yellow), and lettuce (light green).

NEEDLES: US 6 (4mm)

GAUGE: 20 sts/38 rows = 4in (10cm) in garter st

* Make cheese sandwiches for the non-meat eaters.

Directions

Bread:

Work 2 pieces alike. Cast on 2 sts.

Row 1: K1, yo, k1.

Row 2 and every alt row: Purl.

Row 3: K1, m1 (by knitting into the st one row below) k to last st, m1, k1.

Rep rows 3 and 4 until 23 sts, ending with WS row. Bind off.

Ham:

Cast on (approx) 22 sts in pink and work in st st or alternative stitch of choice, until piece measures approx 5in (12cm). Bind off.

Cheese:

Using yellow work as given for ham until piece measures approx 4in (10cm), bind off.

Fold the ham or cheese in half.

Lettuce:

Work 2–3 similar but not necessarily identical pieces. (You don't have to have lettuce if you don't like it!) Using green cast on 3 sts. Work in st st throughout, inc sts irregularly until work measures approx 2in (5cm). Thread yarn through rem sts and pull up and fasten off.

Making up:

Light press or steam pieces (see yarn ball bands). Fold square piece for bread into a triangle from the purl line running on RS of work. Sew sides together. Sew knitted ham or cheese folded in half onto a piece of bread then sew some lettuce leaves on top. Sew another piece of bread on top. Ready to eat!

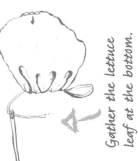

Gather the lettuce leaf at the bottom.

Crochet stout

This is a crochet project, but you can make a lovely pint of stout to share with your friends. Perfect for those occasions when you are the designated driver, or if you are traveling. To make a lighter glass of beer, just choose an appropriate shade of brown to replace the black. You will need a pint glass to work around, but there are usually plenty sitting around in a bar—but do wash it out first, or it will be sticky.

You will need...

MEASUREMENTS: To fit a pint-sized glass

YARN: Sport weight 1 x 1oz (25g) ball in each of black and natural

HOOK: US E (3.5mm)

MATERIALS: 1 pint-sized glass

GAUGE: Not critical

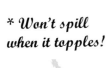

* Won't spill when it topples!

Directions

Round 1: Wind black thread around finger a couple of times and then work 7 sc into thread circle, pull up to close circle.

Round 2: 1ch (as first sc) 1 sc in same place as ch, 2 sc in each st to end, sl st into first ch. 14 sts.

Round 3: 1 ch, *2 sc in next st, 1 sc in next st, rep from * to last st, 2 sc in last st, sl st to ch.

Round 4: 1 ch, *1 sc in next st, 2 sc in next st, 1 sc in next st, rep from * to last st 2 sc in last st, sl st to ch.

Round 5: 1 ch, *1 sc in each of next 2 sts, 2 sc in next st, 1 sc in next st, rep from * to last st 2 sc in last st, sl st to ch.

Continue straight up the glass—fabric should now stretch around glass. Work straight until desired "froth" line reached. Change to natural color and continue straight until cover fits height of glass, fasten off.

Top of glass:

Using natural color work as given for first 4–5 rounds until circle is big enough to cover top of glass. Fasten off.

Making up:

Sew natural circle to top of glass cover (once the glass has been inserted!)

Dinnertime

Vegetables on display bring a kitchen alive, and these ones don't get limp or sprouty, or attract fruit flies. Once you have the knack of vegetable knitting, you could try your hand at carrots, potatoes, tomatoes, or a cauliflower, and start your own market garden. You could even make your own knife and fork.

You will need...

MEASUREMENTS:
Lifelike vegetable sizes

YARN: Pure cotton yarn in sport weight, oddments in a variety of naturalistic colors, i.e. cream, brown, green, in various shades

NEEDLES: US 6 (4mm) and US G6 (4mm) crochet hook

GAUGE: Not required

Directions

Mushroom:

For the cup, 4 sc into a circle (see page 56).

2 sc into every stitch.

1 sc, 2 sc into next stitch repeat* to* the end of this round.

1 sc, 1 sc 2 sc into next stitch repeat * to * to the end of this round.

1 sc into every stitch.

1 sc into every stitch.

1 sc, kip 1 st repeat from * to end the slip last st into the first st. Cut the yarn and draw it out through the last stitch you made to finish.

For the stalk:

4 sc into a circle.

*1 sc, 2 sc into next st * repeat* to * to end.

1 sc into every stitch.

Keep working in around until it gets as long as a stalk.

1 sc, skip 1 repeat * to end.

Fasten off. Attach stalk to center of cup.

✱ *Don't eat the toadstools.*

Onion:

Onion section: Work 4 alike.

Cast on 3 sts please.

Row 1: K1, inc 1, k1, inc1, k1

Row 2, 4, 6, and 8: Purl.

Row 3, 5, and 7: K1, inc1, to last st, inc1, k1.

Work 4 rows st st.

Row 13: K1, sl1, k1, psso, k to last 3 sts, k2 tog, k1.

Row 14: Purl.

Rep last 2 rows until 5 sts rem, ending with RS row.

Work 2 rows in st st.

Next row: K1, sl2, k1, psso, k1. Fasten off.

Onion sprout:

With the same size of needle you used for the onion.

Cast on 2 sts in dark green.

Keep working stockinette sts until it get the required length for the onion you made.

Bind off by knitting 2 sts together. You might need 1 or 2 of them. Sew them on top of the onion!

Making up:

Join onion sections leaving just one seam open at point where they reach the maximum width. Stuff onion with something white, like white stuffing, and sew up the open seam. Onion roots are sewn on with off-white 1 or 2 ply yarn. Sew on as many roots as you like.

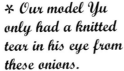
✷ Our model Yu only had a knitted tear in his eye from these onions.

Making the onion

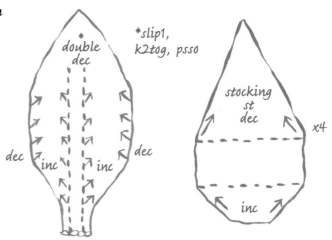

*double dec

**slip1, k2tog, psso

dec   inc   inc   dec

stocking st dec   x4

inc

Ball for the center of lettuce:

Light green sport weight

With US 6 (4mm) needles cast on 6 sts please.

1st row: Increase one in every stitch. (12 sts)

2nd row and every alternate row, purl.

3rd row: (K1, inc. in next st.) 6 times. (18 sts)

5th row: (K2, inc. in next st) 6 times. (24 sts)

7th row: (K3, inc. in next st) 6 times. (30 sts)

9th row: (K3, k2tog) 6 times. (24 sts)

11th row: (K2, k2tog) 6times. (18 sts)

13th row: (K1, k2tog) 6times. (12 sts)

15th row: K2tog to end.

16th row: Purl to end.

Draw up the remaining stitches and sew up the shape, padding it as you go.

Pointy leaves for lettuce:

With green wool, cast on 4 sts.

Keep working on these 4 sts in stockinette sts.

5th row: K1, yrn (to make extra 1stitch) k2, yrn, k1.

6th and every alternate row: P to end.

7th row: K2, yrn, k2, yrn, k2.

9th row: K3, yrn, k2, yrn, k3.

11th row: K4, yrn, k2, yrn, k4.

13th row: K1, sl1, k1, psso, k1, yrn, k2,yrn, k1, k2 tog, k1.

15th row: K1, sl1, k1, psso, k1. yrn, k2, yrn, k1, k2tog, k1.

17th row: K1, sl1, k1, psso, k1, yrn, k2, yrn, k1, k2tog, k1.

19th row: K1, sl1, k1. psso, k to last 3 sts, k2 tog, k1.

21st row: K1, sl1, k1, psso, k to last 3 sts, k2 tog, k1.

23rd row: K1, sl1, k1, psso, k to last 3 sts, k2 tog, k1.

Keep decreasing sts until you get 2sts.

Bind off by K2tog.

Inside leaves:

With light green wool, cast on 10 sts.

1st row: K1, inc1, k to last sts, inc1, k1.

2nd and every alternate row: P to end.

Repeat these 2 rows until you get 20 sts.

10th row: P to end.

11th row: K1, sl1, k1 , psso, k to last 3 sts, k2tog, k1.

12th row: P to end.

Repeat these 2 rows until you get 10 sts left.

Bind off please.

You need 4 or 5 of them to make an organic lettuce!

Making up:

Following the diagrams below, make a central ball that is stuffed, then attach leaves worked in different shades of green around the outside.

Lettuce

Inside leaf

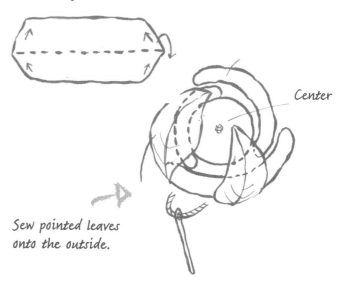

Center

Sew pointed leaves onto the outside.

Chick bootees

Dinner in the oven? Twiddling your thumbs? These chicken bootees can be knitted in the time it takes for your meal to cook. If you are a slow knitter, lower the temperature of your oven. Cook your chicken for 25 minutes per 1lb (500g), plus another 20 minutes if necessary.

You will need...

YARN:
White fingering cotton
1 x 1oz (25g) ball

RECIPE:
1 chicken
stuffing ingredients:-
1oz (25g) butter
1 grated carrot
1 glass of wine
Breadcrumbs (5 slices)
1 tbsp flour
½ pint of stock
Juice of ½ orange
1 tbsp finely chopped orange peel
Salt and pepper to taste

NEEDLES: US 2 (2.75mm)

GAUGE: Not required

NOTE:
Wash your chicken bootees in warm soapy water and use them again and again!

Directions

Preheat the oven to 425°F (220°C/Gas 7). Mix all stuffing ingredients together. Stuff them in the chicken. Baste chicken in oil, season with salt and pepper, and place in the oven.

Cast on 20 sts.

Row 1: Knit into the back of each st.

Starting with a purl row, work in st st (purl 1 row, knit 1 row) until 9 rows have been worked. After 20 mins turn down oven to 375°F (190°C/Gas 5).

Row 10: *K1, m1, rep from * to end.

Row 11: Knit.

Row 12: Knit by wrapping yarn around needle three times to end.

Row 13: Purl by wrapping yarn around needle three times to end. Let go of loops from the last row as you go.

Row 14: K1,* wrap yarn around needle twice, k1* repeat to end.

Row 15: P1, *sl next 5 sts on to RH needle, dropping extra wraps, then slip back on to LH needle, p5tog, rep from * to end. bind off by threading yarn through rem sts.

Finishing:

Pull tight and stitch down side. Press. Test to make sure your chicken is properly cooked by piercing with a fork. If the juice is pink, put it back in the oven for longer. Carefully remove chicken from oven when cooked, using oven gloves, and place bootees where the feet would be.

socks for gardening

frame those precious moments

music with style

House and Garden

knitted mallards

dress to impress

Picture frame

Create family heirlooms by knitting picture frames to decorate photos of your nearest and dearest.

You will need...

MEASUREMENTS:
Window 3½ x 3½in (9 x 9cm), outer
edge, 5½ x 5½in (14 x 14cm)

YARN: Fingering weight Lurex or similar,
1 x 1oz (25g) ball

MATERIALS: Sturdy card 5½ x 5½in
(14 x 14cm)

NEEDLES: US 3 (3.25mm)

GAUGE: Not required

Special notes:

MB = make bobble:

K into front, back, front, back, and front of st—i.e. 5 sts from one.

Work 4 rows on these 5 sts.

Next row: k2tog, k3tog. Insert LH needle into st farthest from needle point and take this st over first (binding off). Bobble completed.

Directions

Frame side: Work 4 alike.

Cast on 35 sts and knit 1 row.

Row 2: *K4, MB, rep from * to end.

Row 3: K2tog, k to last 2 sts, k2tog.

Row 4: P2tog, p to last 2 sts, p2tog.

Rows 5, 6, 7: Work as row 3.

Row 8: Purl.

Making up:

Press each frame side with a cool iron. Arrange into frame shape checking all sides are the same—bobbled edge is the outside of the frame. Stitch the corners together neatly and press again.If you desire a freestanding frame, cut a flap on the back of the card. For a hanging frame, make appropriate holes, thread string through them, and secure with sticky tape. Using craft glue gently stick your photograph to the card. Leave the glue to dry. Glue your knitted frame to the picture and card, taking the edges over the edge of the card, so that the bobbles sit on the outside edge of picture as shown.

5½in sq

Attach your
picture to the
card with glue.

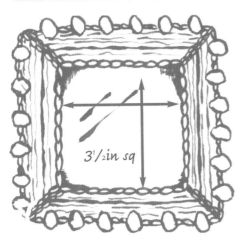

3½in sq

Mitre the corners together.

Hand grenade (a defense against bad television)

Fasten with a kilt pin and key ring! Throw it at the TV—or use it as a handy coin purse.

Directions

Box stitch:

Rows 1–4: *K4, p4 rep from * to end.

Rows 5–8: *P4, k4 rep from * to end.

These 8 rows form patt and are repeated throughout.

Grenade body:

Cast on 40 sts and work in box stitch for 32 rows.

Row 33: Knit.

Row 34: K1, *yrn fwd, k2tog, rep from * to end.

Row 35–39: Knit. Bind off.

Top: RS facing, miss first 5 sts, pick up from 32nd row of grenade body next 30 sts (missing last 5 sts). Using B and starting with a knit row worked 6 rows st st (knit 1 row, purl 1 row) and dec at each end of every purl row.

Row 9: Knit.

Row 10: Purl.

Rep last 2 rows 3 times inc 1 st at each end of purl row. Bind off.

Trigger: Using B Cast on 4 sts. Work in st st starting with a knit row and inc 1 st at each end of knit rows until 4 rows worked. Cont straight in st st for 16 rows. Dec 1 st at each end of every purl row until 2 sts re, K2 tog (1 st).

Make pin loop: Rows 1 and 3: Cast on 1 st.

Rows 2 and 4: Bind off 1 st

Rep these 4 rows until loop measures 1.5in (4cm). Bind off.

You will need...

MEASUREMENTS: 6½in (16.5cm) from top to bottom

YARN: Worsted weight (chunky) acrylic 1 x 1oz (25g) ball in each of green (A) and gray (B)

NEEDLES: US 6 (4mm)

MATERIALS: Stuffing, kilt pin and key ring

GAUGE: Not required

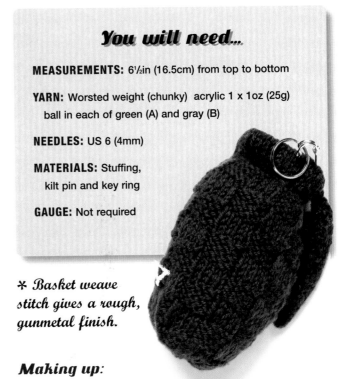

✻ Basket weave stitch gives a rough, gunmetal finish.

Making up:

Press grenade edging and fold along shortest row. Turn a hem, stitching into 32nd row of grenade body. Stitch trigger into a loop. Sew up side of grenade body. Gather the bottom of the grenade by running sts through row 1 of the body and pulling tight. Fold trigger in half lengthwise, press and stitch onto side seam of body with loop at the top. Stuff grenade or, for the purse, gather top opening by running ribbon or narrow elastic through holes made on row 34. Put pin through top and loop—you are ready to throw!

Gauge swatch cardigan

Here's Amy Higgins wearing a cardigan made entirely from gauge swatches. It's a lounging around at home garment, but full of glamour for when unexpected guests arrive. This cardigan is made up of thirty rectangles and four buttons. It's simple to make, easy to wear, and the design is adaptable. We knitted it (mostly) in seed stitch and brick stitches, but the squares can all be different stitches and colors.

You will need...

MEASUREMENTS:

42½in (108cm) One size fits small to large

YARN: Bulky weight silk/alpaca

NEEDLES: US 9 (5.5mm)

MATERIALS: 4 very large buttons

GAUGE: Not specifically required, but each swatch should measure 5½ x 7in (14 x 18cm)

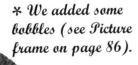

* We added some bobbles (see Picture frame on page 86).

Directions

This swatch cardigan is a good chance to learn about your gauge! The number of stitches and rows you will need to cast on changes depending on the stitch you use. For instance, garter stitch is loose and large, while rib is more elastic so it comes out smaller, and although they are called squares, they will all be rectangular. Use our directions as a guide only as you might work with a slightly different yarn or knit looser or tighter than the original.

Seed stitch swatch:

Cast on 17 sts.

Row 1: *K1, p1, rep from * to end.

Rep this row throughout.

Work approx 37 rows and bind off.

Brick stitch swatch:

Cast on 18 sts.

Row 1: K2, *p2, K2, rep from * to end.

Rows 2 and 3: P2, *k2, p2, rep from * to end.

Row 4: As row 1. Rep these 4 rows throughout and work 36 rows. Bind off.

Making up:

Stitch together 6 rows of 5 pieces placed and sewn as diagram on page 93. Sew on huge buttons as pictured. Rachael's dad made these ones specially. If you can't find any large enough, you can cover a circle of card with a square of knitting gathered around it.

* To make the armholes, sew the first rectangles together where the corners meet..

* Because it is knitted in sections someone else can help you along with it, but then they might want to borrow the cardigan....

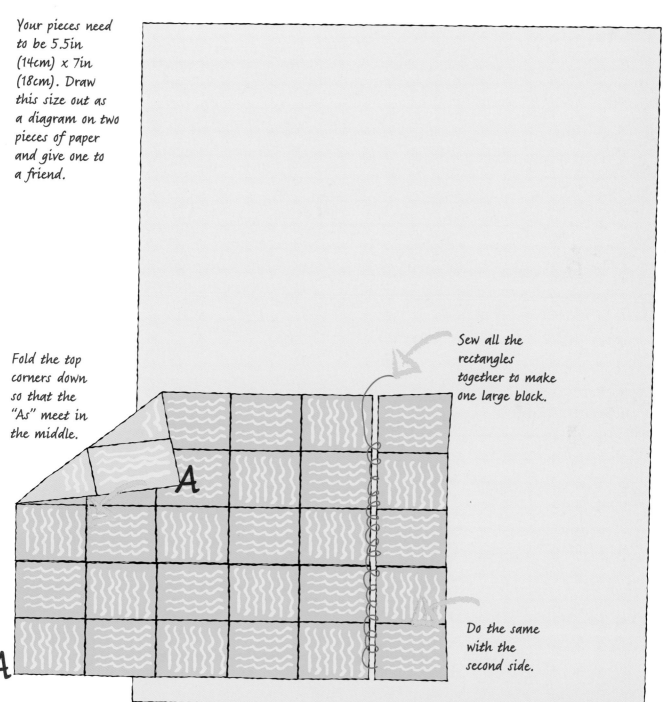

Your pieces need to be 5.5in (14cm) x 7in (18cm). Draw this size out as a diagram on two pieces of paper and give one to a friend.

Fold the top corners down so that the "As" meet in the middle.

Sew all the rectangles together to make one large block.

Do the same with the second side.

Flying ducks

Try a traditional English look for the living room with these knitted mallards. They can be knitted out of scraps of sport weight acrylic that hide in the bottom of yarn stockpiles. Ask your local thrift store. You need a mixture of browns and then a lovely bright yellow, orange, green, and blue.

Directions

No two ducks are the same, so vary the charts on pages 97–101, and use them as a guide to knit different kinds of ducks. The ducks on your local pond might be different to the ones I know. Male ducks seem to be much brighter and well-dressed. (That's Yu in the picture. He's a bit like that too.) Start at the beak and work your way down. The eye is stitched on afterwards. The outer wings are knitted separately and the tail feathers are made with chain stitch. Knitted in acrylic you can machine wash them if they get dusty. Watch them flying around in the tumble dryer.

Main piece head and body

Starting at the beak, cast on 3 sts (this serves as row 1 of chart). Working in st st (so next row will be purl) from chart, inc 1 st at beg of next 2 rows and cont from chart reading RS (knit) rows from R to L and WS (purl) rows from L to R. Use separate balls of yarn for multicolored areas. Where stitches "suddenly appear"—such as in the section immediately after the neck decreases, then they should be cast on. In similar fashion, when a block of stitches "disappear" they should be bound off.

You will need…

MEASUREMENTS: Will depend upon your yarn. Finer yarns will give smaller ducks (you could try a family, work Dad in sports weight, Mom in fingering etc.)

YARN: Oddments in sport weight

NEEDLES: US 6 (4mm)

GAUGE: Not critical

Feet: Using orange, egg yolk yellow, or similar color yarn, cast on 3 sts and work 10 rows st st.

Row 11: K1, inc 1 p-wise, k1, inc 1 p-wise, k1, 5 sts.
Row 12: P1, inc 1 k-wise, k1, p1, k1, inc1 k-wise, p1, 7 sts.
Row 13: K1, inc 1 p-wise, p2, k1, p2, inc 1 p-wise, k1, 9 sts.
Row 14: P1, inc 1 k-wise, k3, p1, k3, inc1 k-wise, p1, 11sts.
Row 15: K1, p4, k1, p4, k1.
Row 16: P1, k4, p1, k4, p1.
Row 17: K1, inc 1 p-wise, p4, k1, p4, inc 1 p-wise, k1, 13 sts.

First toe:

Next row: P1, k3, turn.

Next row: P2tog, p1, k1.

Next row: P1, k2tog.

Next row: P2tog, bind off.

Middle toe:

Next row: K1, p1, k2.

Next row: P2, k1, p2.

Next row: K2tog, p1, k2tog.

Next row: P1, k1, p1.

Next row: Sl1, p2tog, psso, bind off.

Third toe:

Next row: K3, p1.

Next row: K1, p1, p2tog.

Next row: K2tog, p1.

Next row: P2tog, bind off.

Making up:

Press and darn in all ends.

Sew to main body of duck as shown.

Outer wing

This diagram represents the outer part of the wing.

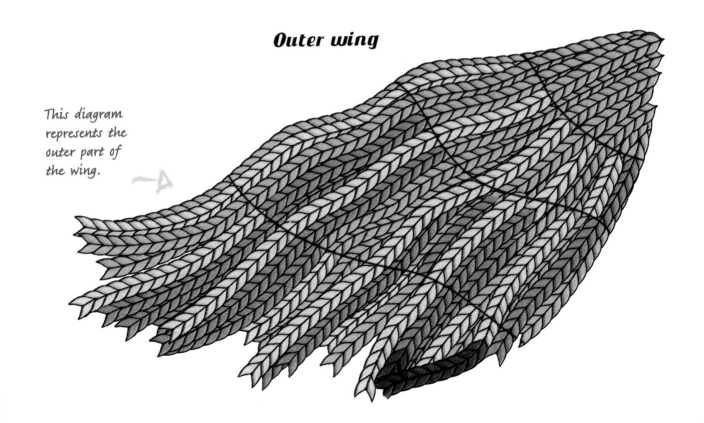

Duck chart overview

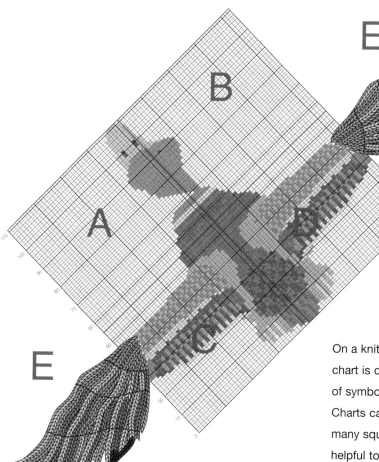

TIP
This is one of those projects where you are managing lots of colors at once. Cut off a short length of each colored yarn and make a bobbin (see page 15).

On a knitting chart, each square represents one stitch. The chart is drawn as the front. There will sometimes be a code of symbols representing all the different colors or stitches. Charts can appear overwhelming because there are so many squares to look at. If this is the case it might be helpful to photocopy the chart, and then cross off the rows with a pencil as you finish them. This way you don't get lost. If you are using a lot of colors, take a snip of each one, and stick it to your chart key to avoid confusion later.

It is usual to begin a chart at the lower right-hand corner, knitting the odd rows (like row 1), and purling the even rows if you are working in stockinette stitch. If you work from left to right, all the patterns and shapings will be reversed, which could be a good thing, unless you are copying letters, in which case they will come out back to front.

Understanding knitting charts

Parts of this book use knitting charts instead of the old fashioned written pattern. This is easier to read when knitting intarsia (color work) or working cables. Charts are often easier than a written pattern because you can see the shape of the garment and visualize the patterns you are making.

Chart A

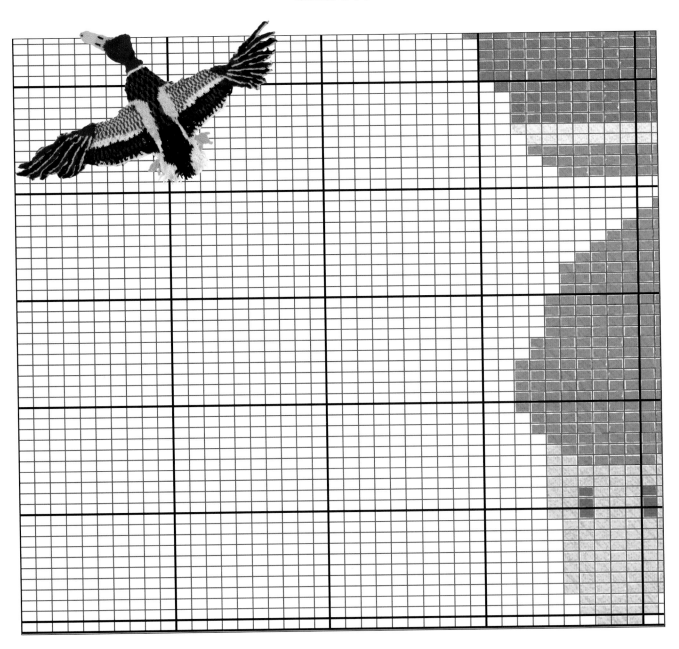

Chart B

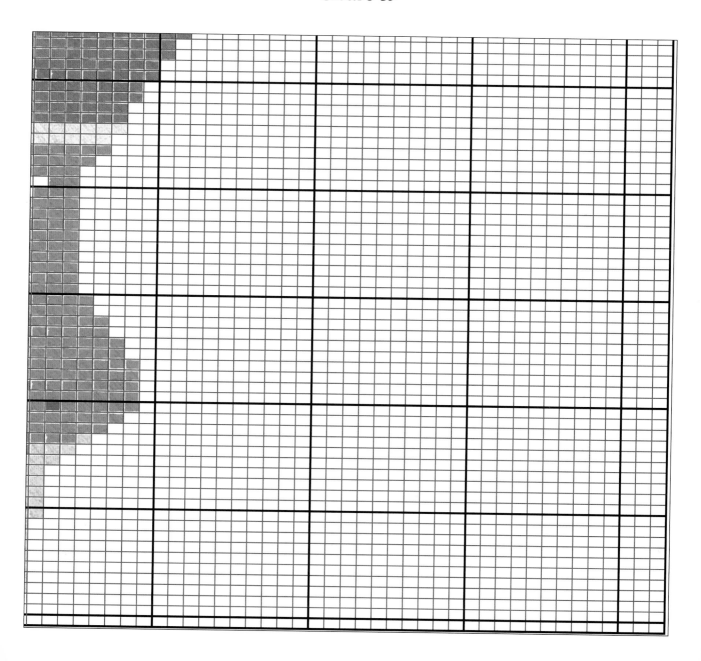

Chart C

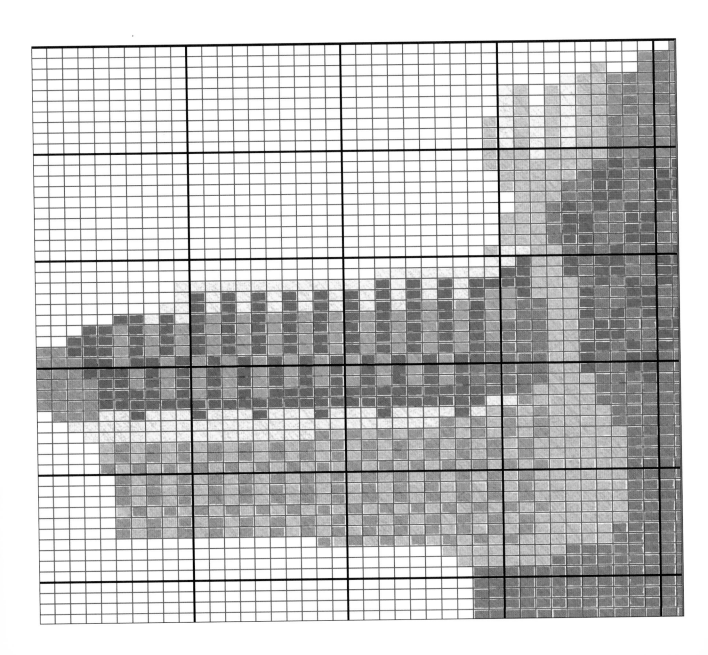

Chart D

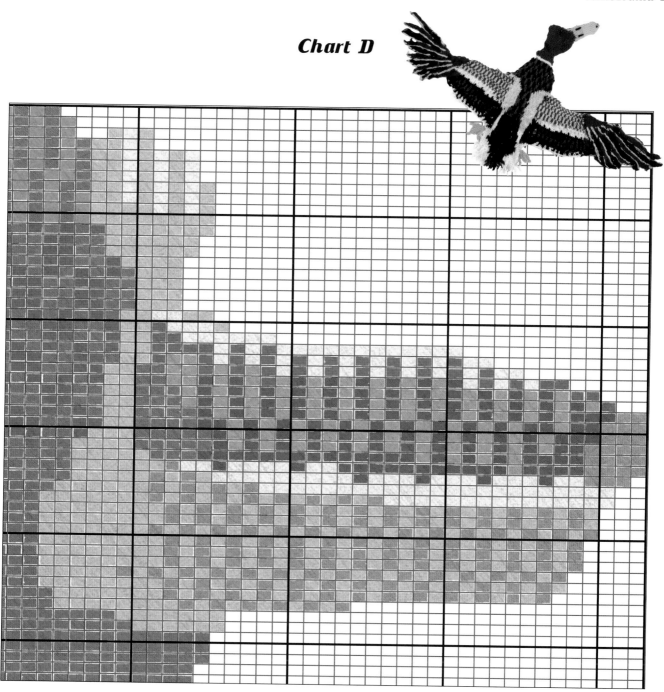

Patio socks

Annie doesn't actually have a patio, because she lives in a top-floor apartment, but if she did these are the socks she would wear for watering the plants. Patio socks are knitted on two needles in kid mohair with lots of little knitted flowers and vines stitches on top. You can knit as many flowers as you like in all different colors and let them fall over the top of your boots and wrap around your feet. Knit elastic into the rib for extra tightness.

You will need...

MEASUREMENTS: Foot length approx 8in (20.5cm). One size fits small to large

YARN: Fingering silk/mohair 2 x 1oz (50g) balls in natural (A), oddments in green (B), pinks (C), gold (D), and brown (E)

NEEDLES: US 3 (3.25mm) and US D (3mm) crochet hook

MATERIALS: Knitting elastic to match (optional)

GAUGE: 19 sts and 30 rows to 4in (10cm)

Directions

Work 2 alike.

Using A cast on 49 sts. Run knitting elastic in with A and work 12 rows k1, p1 rib. Drop elastic and cont working in A alone. Start and work in st st (k1 row, p1 row) throughout and work until sock measures 7in (18cm) ending with WS row. Break yarn.

Heel:

Slip 12 sts on to RH needle, slip next 24 sts on to a stitch holder, slip rem 13 sts onto a spare needle, turn. With WS facing rejoin yarn to instep edge of 12 sts at the end of the row and purl to last st, turn needle around with WS facing, p2tog (last st on RH needle and first st on spare needle), p to end. 24 sts. Work 10 rows st st.

Turn heel:

Next Row: K13, sl 1, k1, psso, k1, turn.

Next Row: P4, p2tog, p1, turn.

Next Row: K5, sl 1, k1, psso, k1 turn.

Next Row: P6, p2tog, p1, turn.

Keep dec as set until 14 sts rem ending with WS row and break off yarn. RS facing, rejoin yarn to instep, pick up, and k10 sts evenly alongside of heel, k across 14 sts of heel, pick up, and k10 sts evenly along other side of heel. 34 sts.

Shape instep:

Row 1: Purl to end.

Row 2: K1, sl 1, k1, psso, k to last 3 sts, k2tog, k1.

Rep last 2 rows 4 times then first row once. 24 sts. *Work straight until foot measures 6in (15cm) ending with WS row.

Shape toe:

Row 1: K3, sl 1, k1, psso, k to last 5 sts, k2tog, k3.

Row 2: Purl to end.

Rep last 2 rows 4 times. 14 sts. Break off yarn*.

With RS facing rejoin yarn to 24 sts left on stitch holder and rep from * to *. Graft sts together from both needles (see page 37).

Making up:

Join leg and foot seams. Press work gently.

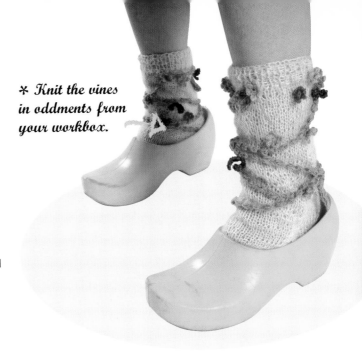

✻ *Knit the vines in oddments from your workbox.*

Flowers: Work quite a few in a selection of C and D. Cast on using C or D, 4 sts. *Bind off 2 of these sts (leaving 1 st each on RH and LH needle). Transfer the st to LH needle. Rep from * 5 more times and bind off all stitches. Sew both ends together to form a flower.

Leaves: Work as many as desired using B. Cast on 3 sts and knit to end.

Row 2 and alt rows: Purl

Row 3: K1, yo, k1, yo, k1.

Row 5: K2, yo, k1, yo, k2.

Row 7: K2tog, yo, k1, yo, k2tog.

Row 9: K1, sl2, k1, psso, k1.

Row 10: Break off thread leaving approx 3in (8cm), thread through needle and then through rem sts, pull up and fasten off.

Crocheted vine

1. Using B, work 1 ch.

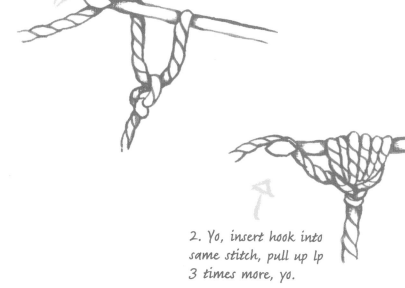

2. Yo, insert hook into same stitch, pull up lp 3 times more, yo.

3. Draw through all 1ps on hook, 1 ch, and repeat.

Crocheted Leaves:

Using E work 6 ch. 1 dc in 2nd ch from hook, htr into next ch, tr into next ch, htr into next ch, dc into next ch and sl st into same ch.

You can work 2 leaves in one go if you recommence a leaf immediately after completing one without fastening off the yarn. Vary the size of leaves by changing the number of chains and working more tr at the center.

Crocheted vine:

Using B, work 1 ch. *Yo, pull up lp loosely—approx ½in (1.5cm), yo insert hook into same st, pull up lp 3 times more, yo, draw through all lps on hook, 1ch.

Rep from * until vine is long enough to creep up your socks as shown.

Making up:

Sew the vines onto the socks, arranging as desired. Sew a selection of flowers and leaves close to the vines as shown.

Speaker covers

Why are speaker covers always gray or black? How about fitting them in with your home décor? Most speakers have a detachable front that consists of a frame with a thin mesh cover. Rip the mesh off and knit a cover for the frame! These covers are best suited to the more experienced knitter—casting on, and the first few rounds, are a bit of a challenge, so we suggest you sit at a table with good lighting to start off. If you have time you could crochet or knit around the speaker cable too!

You will need...

MEASUREMENTS:
As shown approx 19 x 9in (48.5 x 23cm) woofer approx 8½in (22cm) diameter and tweeter approx 4½in (11cm) diameter. Easily adjusted to fit your own speakers

YARN: Fingering Lurex 2 x 1oz (25g) balls in each of gold (A) and blue (B)

NEEDLES: 5 x US 8 (5mm) double pointed and a pair of US 15 (10mm)

MATERIALS: 1½yd (1m) black iron-on interfacing (or size to fit the speaker frame)

GAUGE: Not required—stitches will be loose as needles are quite large for the yarn thickness

Directions

Overview:

Speakers are made using the "rays" method of forming a circle. For those of you into math, it was invented by Elizabeth Zimmerman in 1969 and is based on the formula for circumference: $C = \pi r^2$. Instead of working increases along lines that radiate out from the center, like other Shetland rounds, she increases in rounds to form a sequence of circles within circles, like the diagram on the following page. Each circle represents an increase round, in which the stitch numbers are doubled. So the number of stitches on each increase round is doubled and the distance between each increase round is double the distance between the last two increase rounds. This produces flat lying circles, where you can change color and stitches as you please. Our tweeters and woofers were knitted in stockinette stitch and garter stitch but yours can change depending on how brave you are! Shetland Rounds are worked using five double pointed needles and are a variation on a pattern by Martha Waterman in *Traditional Knitted Lace Shawls* (Interweave Press).

Woofer:

Using A, cast on 2 sts onto each of 4 needles (8 sts in total). Knit with the fifth needle. Place a marker and join, being careful not to twist the sts (it gets easier as the sts increase!).

Rnd 1: Knit

Rnd 2: *Inc 1, k1, rep from * 16 sts.

Rnds 3, 4 and 5: Knit

Rnd 6: *Inc 2, k1, rep from * 48 sts.

Rnd 7: Using B, purl.

Rnd 8: Knit.

Rnd 9: Using A, purl.

Rnd 10: *Inc 2, k3, rep from * to end, 80 sts.

Rnd 11, 12 and 13: Knit.

Rnd 14: *Inc 2, k5, rep from * to end, 112 sts.

Rnd 15, 16, and 17: Knit.

Rnd 18: *Inc 2, k7, rep from * to end. 144 sts.

Rnd 19: Using B, purl.

Rnd 20: Knit

Rnd 21: Using A, purl.

Rnd 22: Bind off.

For bigger woofers continue increasing 2 sts 16 times every 4th round and working 2 more knit sts between increase points each increase round.

Tweeter:

Work as given for woofer to round 9.

Rnd 10: Bind off.

Mesh:

Using US 15 (10mm) needles and B, cast on 30 sts. Knit until piece is long enough to completely cover speaker frames and overlap a little at each edge. Bind off.

Making up:

Cut iron-on interfacing to size to fit over speaker and lap over frame edges at back. Miter corners. Stretch knitting over the ironing board and pin it down to shape. Place interfacing, glue side down on top of knitting, and press. (You might want to protect your ironing board with baking parchment—or something that will protect the surface and yet not allow glue to stick to it—test a small piece beforehand). Stitch, pin, or tape onto speaker cover. Pin woofers and tweeters in position and slip stitch in position. If you have time, you could crochet or knit around the speaker cables. They look lovely draped across your carpet.

Circle shaping

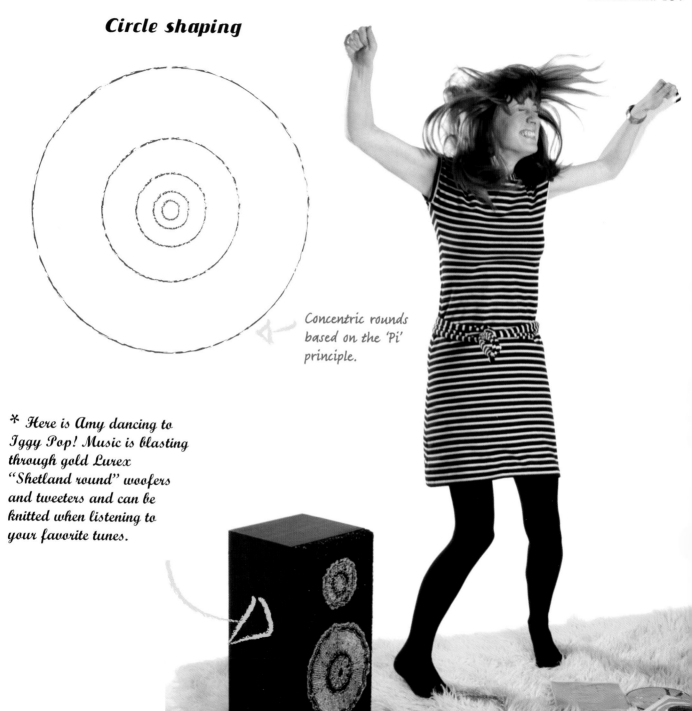

Concentric rounds based on the 'Pi' principle.

＊ Here is Amy dancing to Iggy Pop! Music is blasting through gold Lurex "Shetland round" woofers and tweeters and can be knitted when listening to your favorite tunes.

knitted lingerie will keep you warm with style

wake up in style with a flapper nightie

black out the outside world

Bedside Table

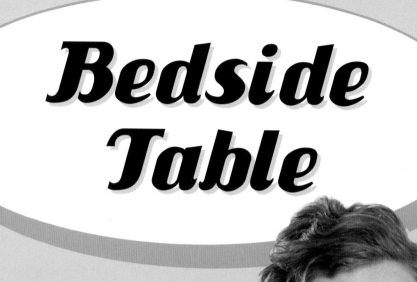

exfoliate with the best of them…

keep warm on the high seas

Sponge cover

Select the appropriate yarn for your sponge cover, and your bath or shower can be as invigorating or relaxing as you desire. The nylon string used on our sponge makes a super-exfoliating version. A quick scrub with this in the shower and you will revive the circulation to your extremities.

You will need...

MEASUREMENTS:
5 x 3 x 1½in (13 x 7.5 x 4cm)
(easily adaptable)

YARN: Sport weight nylon string 1 ball
in each of 2 colors

NEEDLES: US 6 (4mm)

MATERIALS: Bath sponge of same
or slightly smaller measurements
as cover

GAUGE: Not required

Directions

Use two strands, one of each color, together throughout.

Back and front: Work 2 pieces alike.

Cast on 10 sts and knit 36 rows. Bind off.

Top and sides: Cast on 4 sts and knit 88 rows. Bind off.

Making up:

Wrap the circumference around the side edge of sponge and sew together using one end of the string. Sew front and then back on around sponge at each side. We recommend that you wash with warm soapy water!

* *The pretty variegated effect is made by using two strands at once.*

PLEASE NOTE:
*Don't scrub too hard,
or you will rub off too
much skin.*

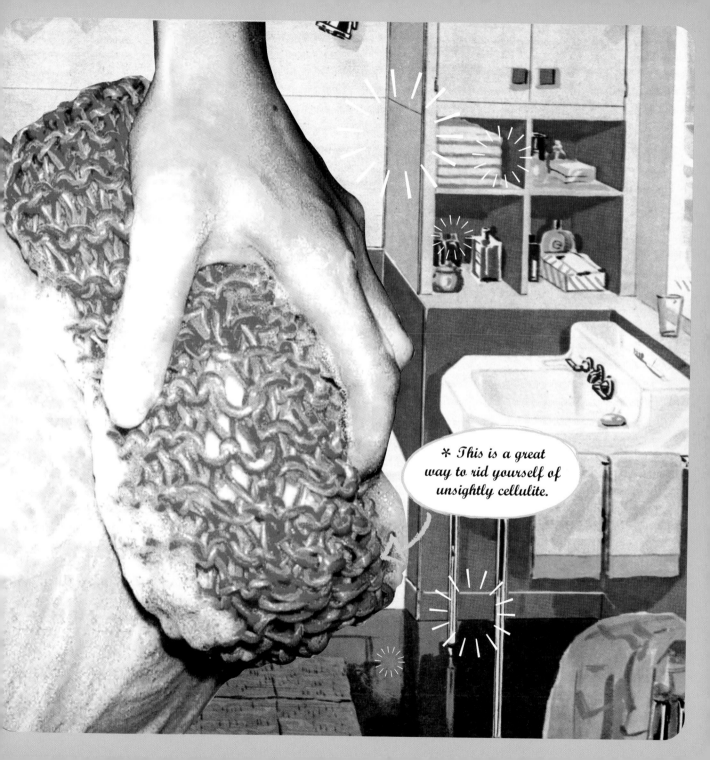

Blindfold

For resting, dreaming, and other pleasures, a knitted blindfold is a great accessory for getting away from it all. Knitted in black sport weight, the main body can be lined for extra comfort and blindness—just knit it twice! That's me trying to sleep in an uncomfortable position.

You will need...

MEASUREMENTS:
To fit your head

YARN: Sport weight
cotton 1 x 1oz (25g)
(add fine silvery
thread for glitter
effect)

NEEDLES: US 3
(3.25mm)

MATERIALS: Elastic
to suit

GAUGE: Not required

Directions

Cast on 6 sts and knit 1 row. Inc 1 st at each end of next and every foll alt row until 14 sts. Knit 1 row.

Row 10: Knit to end, cast on 2 sts and cut thread.

Work a second piece up to row 9.

Row 10: Cast on 2 sts and knit to end.

Put 2 sides of the blindfold together with newly cast on sts in the middle (32 sts).

Rows 11–16: Knit placing markers at each end of 16th row (safety pins will do).

Row 17: K2tog, k28, k2tog

Row 18: Knit.

Row 19: K2tog, k26, k2tog.

Row 20: K12, slip rem sts onto a needle.

Left side:

Row 21: K2tog, k8, k2tog.

Row 22: Knit.

Row 23: K2tog, k6, k2tog.

Row 24: Bind off.

Right side:

Row 21: Bind off 6 sts, k8, k2tog.

Row 22: Knit.

Row 23: K2tog, k6, k2tog.

Row 24: Bind off.

Edging:

RS facing pick up 35 sts around top side of blindfold from marker to marker.

Row 1: Purl inc 7 sts evenly along the row.

Row 2: Knit. **Row 3:** Purl.

Row 4: K1, *yrn, yfwd, k2tog, rep from * to end.

Row 5: Purl. **Row 6:** Knit.

Row 7: Purl.

Row 8: Bind off.

The 4th row forms the edge of the blindfold. Fold, press and hem.

Underside:

Pick up 48 sts.

Row 1: Purl, inc 1 st every 4 sts—12 inc in all.

Rows 2–8: Work as edging and fasten off.

Making up:

Thread elastic through twice in same position as markers. Adjust to fit your head, and secure.

Hot water bottle cover

That is Stephen, warm in a storm on one of his expeditions. It's easy these days to be seduced by fluffy yarns for comfort, but this is made with pure Swaledale Aran which is tough and really warm. Rough organic yarns smell lovely and woolly when the bottle gets hot. When prepared, they retain their natural oils, making the wool water resiliant. This will keep Stephen warm longer, wherever he is. The bottle is covered in a twisted cable turtleneck, with a brick stitch cardigan on top for cold fingers and toes. Slip your toes into the cardigan if they get chilly.

You will need...

MEASUREMENTS:
To suit an average hot water bottle

YARN: Bulky Swaledale wool
3 x 4oz (3 x 100g) balls.

NEEDLES: US 8 (6mm)

MATERIALS: 1 medium-sized hot
water bottle; 3 leather woven buttons

GAUGE: Not critical

PLEASE NOTE:
To wash, put the cover and bottle in the washing machine in a cool, gentle wash. Refill the bottle with hot water and leave until dry.

Pattern notes:

1 x 1 rib:
RS rows: *K1, p1, rep from * to end.
WS rows: *K1, p1, rep from * to end.

Cable worked thus:
Working over the K4 sts on RS rows (see 4 x 2 rib directions), slip next 2 sts onto a cable needle and hold at front of work. Knit next 2 sts, k2 from cable needle. For step-by-steps see page 34.

Basketwork pattern: (6 st repeat)
Rows 1–3: *k3, p3 rep from to end.
Rows 4–6: *p3, k3 rep from * to end

Directions

Cover: Work back and front alike: (Begins at turtleneck): Cast on 26 sts and work 30 rows k1, p1 rib. Begin the cable pattern, working increases and pattern repeats as shown on the chart, until you have worked cable twist row 8 times. Keeping 4 x 2 patt correct as set, dec 1 st at each end

of next row, work 1 row. Dec 1 st at each end of next 3 rows. Work 1 row and bind off. Make 2.

Cardigan back:

Cast on 26 sts and work 2 rows 1x1 rib. Inc 1 st at each end of next 2 rows. 30 sts. Start and work in basketwork patt (see patt note) throughout work 1 row. Increase 1 st at each end—taking inc sts into patt—until 36 sts. Cont straight until 62 rows basketwork worked. Dec 1 st at each end of next 2 rows. Dec 2 sts at each end of next 2 rows. bind off rem sts.

Right front:

Cast on 18 sts and work 2 rows 1x1 rib. Keeping rib patt correct as set, inc 1 st at end (side edge) of next row. Inc 1 st at beg of next row and work in rib to last 5 sts. Bind off over next 3 sts, work last 2 sts rib.

Next row: Work 2 sts rib as set, cast on 3 sts over sts bound off in last row (forms buttonhole), work to end, inc 1 st. Work 1 row, inc 1 st at end of next row. Start and work in basketwork patt (see patt notes), commencing with inc 1 st at this edge and k1 st then work patt repeat to last 7 sts, work these in 1x1 rib as set. Keeping 7 sts in rib at front edge as now set throughout, cont to inc 1 st at side edge until 23 sts, taking new st into basketwork patt. *Work straight for 14 rows, work buttonhole on straight rib edge over same sts as before over next 2 rows. Rep from * once more, ending on WS row (work extra row if required).

Cable chart

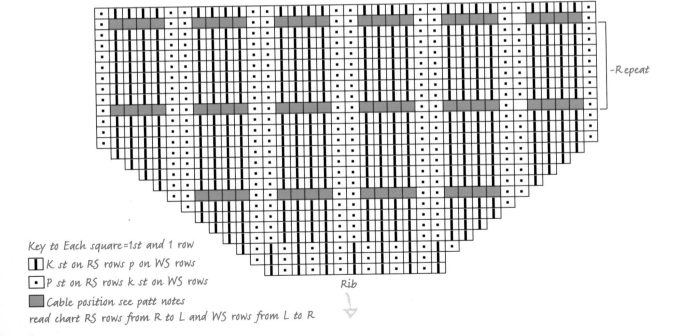

Key to Each square=1st and 1 row
☐ K st on RS rows p on WS rows
• P st on RS rows k st on WS rows
▓ Cable position see patt notes
read chart RS rows from R to L and WS rows from L to R

-Repeat

Rib

Shape neck: **Work 5 sts 1x1 rib, k2tog, cont in basketwork patt as set to end. Work 1 row**. Rep from ** to ** until 11 sts remain. Keeping front neck 5 sts in 1x1 rib as set and remainder in basketwork as far as possible, dec 1 st at side edge on each row and 1 st at neck edge (5 sts in as before) on alt rows until 5 sts rem, bind off.

Left front: Work as given for right front reversing, shaping, and omitting buttonholes.

Pockets: Make two. Cast on 9 sts and work 4 rows 1x1 rib. Work 6 rows basketwork stitch and bind off.

Making up:

Join bottle cover seams, leaving a big enough gap to fit in hot water bottle. Insert hot water bottle and join seams up to turtleneck. Join turtleneck seams, remembering to reverse them at halfway fold point. Set pockets in position on cardigan fronts. Join shoulder and side seams of cardigan. Sew on buttons to correspond with buttonholes. These brown leather woven buttons are traditional for an Aran cardigan.

Plan of hot water bottle cover

Turn the neck down at the top.

This is the cardigan for the outside.

✻ You can put your cold hands inside the cardigan.

Garter

Here is Rosie modeling the garter. Isn't she beautiful? We were discussing what a garter is for because you usually have just one, so it's not technically for holding up stockings. So apart from being beautiful, we suggest you use it for all sorts of things like holding shopping lists or, knitted in blue, it would make the perfect gift for a girlfriend getting married. The garter is made up of two edging techniques, triangular garter edging and bobble edging. The spool knitted ribbons are finished with foxglove petal shapes. Elastic can be added when threading the ribbons, but this is optional.

You will need...

MEASUREMENTS: 13½ x 3in (34 x 7.5cm) One size fits all

YARN: Fingering silk 1 x 1oz (25g) ball in each of natural (A) and blue (B)

NEEDLES: US 6 (4mm)

MATERIALS: Spool knitting bobbin

GAUGE: Not required

TIP:
Try out the new stitches with an oddment of yarn, so as not to waste the lovely silk.

Directions

Pattern note:

K into front, back, front, back, and front of st—i.e. 5 sts from one. Work 4 rows on these 5 sts.

Next row: k2tog, k3tog. Insert LH needle into st furthest from needle point and take this st over first (binding off). Bobble completed.

Triangular edging:

Using A cast on 7 sts.

Row 1: K2, yo, k2tog, k to end.

Row 2: Knit

Rows 3–15: Rep rows 1 and 2 6 times more then rep row 1.

Rows 16: Bind off 8 sts and K to end.

Rep these 16 rows 10 times. Bind off.

This edging makes 2 rows of holes which you will thread the spool knitting through later.

Bobble edging:

Pick up sts along the straight top edge of the triangular edging, one st for each row (160 sts).

Row 1: Knit.

Row 2: K5, MB, rep to end.

Row 3: K2, MB, k5, rep to end pushing bobbles through to the other side. Bind off.

Ribbons:

Use a spool knitter and B to work ribbons approx 32in (81cm) and 27in (68.5cm) long.

Petal ends:

Using B, cast on 15 sts.

Row 1: Knit.

Row 2: Purl, dec 1 st at each end of row.

Rep these 2 rows until 5 sts rem.

Don't bind off, just take the sts and sew them into the end of the spool knitting subtly so that the flower looks like it is graduating into a stalk.

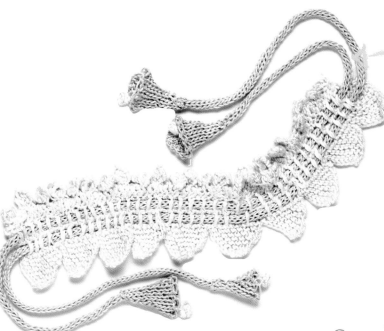

✱ *These are the spool-
knitted ribbons. In the
UK it is known as
French knitting,
appropriate for lingerie.*

Stamen:

Work 4 alike.

Using A, cast on one st. Knit into back, front, back, and front of this st (4 inc made). Knit 4 rows, lift 3 sts over the first st, and tie the 2 ends, fasten off leaving a short length.

Making up:

Stitch down the sides of the flower and give it a tug so that it looks a bit like a foxglove petal. Finish stamens by snipping off one end and stitching the other end into the petal and make sure the stamen hangs out of the petal and dangles a bit.

Spool knitting

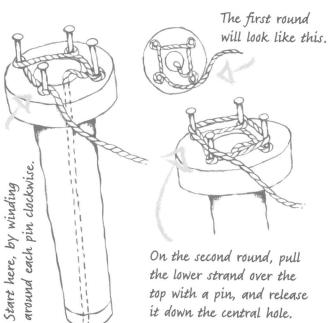

*The first round
will look like this.*

Start here, by winding around each pin clockwise.

*On the second round, pull
the lower strand over the
top with a pin, and release
it down the central hole.*

Knitted lingerie

There is nothing as seductive as the tickle of kid mohair. This luxurious yarn is taken from the first shearing of the youngest goats, which is extra soft on the skin. The mohair is quite fragile, so here it has been mixed with silk for added strength. Don't be daunted by the lacy butterfly pattern. If you haven't knitted a lace stitch before, this is a good one to start with, and if you make a mistake, no one will ever see it.

You will need...

MEASUREMENTS: To fit 32–36in (81–91cm) hip

YARN: Sport weight kid mohair 1 x 1oz (25g) ball in each of plum and natural

NEEDLES: US 7 (4.5mm), size F (4mm) crochet hook

MATERIALS: Waist length of narrow elastic

GAUGE: 20 sts and 22 rows to 4in (10cm) using US 7 (4.5mm) needles measured over lace pattern

Knitting note: Increases and decreases worked 1 st in—i.e. inc (or dec) actually done on 2nd st from each edge.

Special abbreviation: wyb = with yarn in back

Directions

Front:

Using plum cast on 20 sts. Start and work in lace patt (see diagram on page 127) throughout, setting it up thus:

Row 1: K1, k2tog, yo, k1, yo, ssk (slip 2 sts k-wise then insert tip of L needle into the front of these 2 sts and knit them tog tbl with the R needle) k5, k2tog, yo, k1, ssk, k4.

Cont in patt as set throughout, taking extra sts into patt repeat and at the same time, inc 1 st at each side of next 11 rows.

Leg opening increases: Cast on 5 sts at each end of next row, work 1 row. Cast on 4 sts, at each end of next row, work 1 row. Cast on 7 sts at each end of next row, purl 1 row. Cast on 5 sts, at each end of next row, work 1 row. Cast on 3 sts, at each end of next row, work 1 row. Cast on 7 sts at each end of next row, work 2 rows. Dec 1 st at each end of next row, work 3 rows. Dec 1 st at each end of next row, work 2 rows. Dec 1 st at each end of next and foll alt row, work 10 rows. Dec 1 st at each end of next and foll alt row, work 7 rows. Work 6 rows st st as set. Purl 1 row. Work 4 rows st st and bind off.

Back:

Using plum, cast on 36 sts. Start and work in patt throughout, arranging patt repeat thus:

Row 1: K1, *k2tog, yo, k1, yo, ssk, k5, rep from * twice, k2tog, yo, k1, yo ssk.

Always taking inc sts into patt repeat, inc 1 st at each end of next 4 rows, purl 1 row. Inc1 st at each end of next 5 rows, purl 1 row. Cast on 5 sts, patt to end, cast on 5 sts, work 1 row. Cast on 4 sts, patt to end, cast on 4 sts, work 1 row. Cast on 7 sts, k to end, cast on 7 sts, purl 1 row. Cast on 8 sts, patt to end, cast on 8 sts. Work 3 rows. Dec 1 st at each end of next row, work 5 rows. Dec 1 st at each end of next row, work 3 rows. Dec 1 st at each end of next and foll alt row, work 17 rows. Dec 1 st at each end of next row, work 3 rows. Dec 1 st at each end of next row, work 3 rows. Work 4 rows st st as set. Purl 2 rows. Work 4 rows st st and bind off.

Gusset:

Using plum cast on 36 sts and knit 1 row.

Row 2: P1, sl1, p1, psso, p to last 3 sts, p2tog, p1.

Row 3: K1, sl1, k1, psso, k to last 3 sts, k2tog, k1.

Row 4: Purl.

Rep last 2 rows 7 times.

Row 19: K1, sl1, k1, psso, k to last 3 sts, k2tog, k1.

Work 5 rows st st ending WS row.

Row 25: K1, inc 1, k to last st, inc 1, k1.

Work 3 rows st st.

Row 29: As row 25.

Work 3 rows st st and bind off.

Making up:

Sew gusset to front and back pieces respectively. Join side seams. Turn over top for hem and slip stitch down leaving a small opening for waist elastic. Thread elastic through waistband, adjust to fit, and fasten off securely. Complete waist hem. Finish leg openings using US F (4mm) crochet hook and contrast yarn and with RS facing, work 1 row of double crochet around each leg edge. Fasten off and neaten ends.

Making the elastic casing

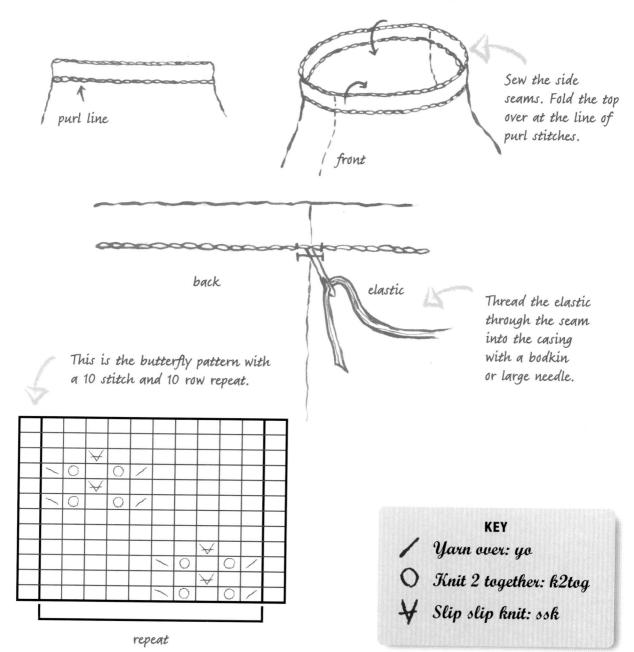

purl line

Sew the side seams. Fold the top over at the line of purl stitches.

front

back

elastic

Thread the elastic through the seam into the casing with a bodkin or large needle.

This is the butterfly pattern with a 10 stitch and 10 row repeat.

repeat

KEY

/ Yarn over: yo

O Knit 2 together: k2tog

⋎ Slip slip knit: ssk

Big-night-out bra

This gorgeous bra is taken from an old 1930s knitting pattern, and is knitted in silk. It has a relaxed support and is warm and pretty. Here, Rachael is getting ready for her big Saturday night out with the girls, and the phone just won't stop ringing.

You will need...

MEASUREMENTS: To fit 34[36]in (81[86]cm) bust

YARN: Fingering silk 2 x 1oz (50g) balls in cream

NEEDLES: US 0 and US 2 (2mm and 3.25mm)

MATERIALS: 2 hooks and eyes, 1yd (1m) ribbon for straps (optional)

GAUGE: 28 sts to 4in (10cm) measured over st st on US 2 (3.25mm) needles

Directions

Center:

Work 2 pieces alike. Instructions in [ ] are for larger size bra.

Using US 0 (2mm) needles, cast on 138[168] sts.

Row 1: *K21[26], yf, k2tog, rep from * to end.

Row 2 and all alt rows: Purl

Row 3: *K19[24], k2tog, yf, k2tog, rep from * to end.

Row 5: *K18[23], k2tog, yf, k2tog, rep from * to end.

Row 7: *K17[22], k2tog, yf, k2tog, rep from * to end.

Row 9: *K16[21], k2 tog, yf, k2tog, rep from * to end.

Row 11: *K15[20], k2tog, yf, k2tog, rep from * to end.

Cont to dec as set on alt rows, working 1 st less before each dec until 18 [24] sts rem. Purl 1 row. Break off yarn leaving a tail approx 6in (12.5cm) long. Thread end through sewing needle and needle through rem sts, pull up and fasten off securely.

PLEASE NOTE:
*Use a soft natural yarn
to wear next to your skin.
This fine silk is ideal.*

Band:

Work 2 pieces alike.

Using US 0 (2mm) needles cast on 9 sts and work in moss st thus:

Pattern Row: *K1, p1, rep from * to last st, k1.

Rep this row until band measures approx 34[38]in (86[91]cm) and bind off.

Making up:

Lightly steam work on the wrong side. Join side seams of bra pieces. Join the side edges of the bands together for approx 4[5]in (10[13]cm). Cross the 2 bands and pin together at their centers. Place 1 (round) center piece between the bands and stitch 1 band along the top edge and the second band along the lower edge, bringing the bands together again in the center. Now stitch the bands round the second center, keeping the crossover at center front so that you will stitch the band from the lower edge of the first center piece along the top edge of the second center piece and vice versa. Bring the bands together again in the center cross and stitch together along the side edges to form the other end of the back strap. Sew two eyes to one strap, adjust to fit and sew on hooks to correspond on other strap. Add ribbon shoulder straps, and adjust to fit.

✻ *Rachael is getting ready for her big night out!*

Making up the bra

Pieces fit
together
like this.

Sew eyes to
one end of
the straps.

Sew hooks to
the other end.

Use silk thread
to sew together.

Flapper nightdress

Naomi has been working so hard at the hairdressers. She has to get up early every morning, including Saturdays. When she gets home late, all she wants to do is flop in front of the television and knit backwards and forwards in stockinette stitch. This nightdress can be knitted with little concentration, because you can drop as many stitches as you like, forming ladders. Every fifth row, you can wrap the yarn around the needle more than once, making it grow faster, with less effort! Finished with a simple edging and shiny ribbons, Naomi rises every morning feeling sexy and looking amazing.

You will need...

MEASUREMENTS:
To fit 32-42in (81-106cm) bust

YARN: Fingering cotton 9 x 1oz (25g) balls in white

NEEDLES: US 6 (4mm)

MATERIALS: Approx 4yd (3.5m) narrow ribbon in 2 colors

GAUGE: Not required

Directions

Border triangle: Work 8 alike.

Cast on 2 sts.

Row 1: Knit through back of loop.

Row 2 and all alt rows: Purl.

Row 3: K1, yo, k1.

Row 5: K1, inc 1 by knitting into st one row below, k to last st, inc 1, k1.

Rep 2nd and 5th row until you have 23 sts, slip these onto a stitch holder (or large safety pin).

Elongated stitch

Wrap the yarn around the needle twice first.

Next row just make one stitch.

Front:

Slip 4 triangles from stitch holder onto needle. *Knit 4 rows st st. Knit 1 row wrapping yarn around needle 3 times on each st. Knit 4 rows st st. Knit 1 row wrapping yarn around the needle twice on each st. Rep from * until front reaches just over bust line (whatever length you prefer, nightie shown measured 31in (79cm) from tip of point).

From the bust line onwards it is time to start making ladders. Make as many ladders as you dare. Naomi laddered every 15 sts, that being her choice. The combination of big stitches and ladders makes a chequered effect. Knit a little sample if you are unsure, but go for it, it's a great feeling to drop stitches after all that hard work!

Shape neck:

You should have 92 sts**. K46 and slip rem 46 sts on to a stitch holder. Cont in patt as set and dec 1 st (1 stitch in from the edge for neatness) at each end of row until 2 sts rem. Bind off.

Slip rem 46 sts back on to needle and work as given for first side.

Eyelet edging:

RS facing, pick up evenly and knit sts from top of front, then purl 1 row.

***Next Row:** *K2, k2tog, yo, rep from * to end.

Next Row: Purl.

Rep last 2 rows once more. Bind off.

Front and back of nightdress

This is the eyelet edging for the ribbon on the front.

These are the eyelets at the top for the ribbon on the back.

This is the triangular border.

1   2   3   4

Back:

Work as given for front to **. Work 2 rows st st and then work eyelet edging from *** to end.

Making up:

Sew side seams. Using a length of each color ribbon together, thread eyelets at top edge, adjust to fit, and tie in bows as shown.

✶ The long stitches make this very quick to knit up.

Pesky conversions

In an ideal world, we would all use the same measurements, but of course, things are never that simple.

Yarn information

US	UK	AUS
Fingering	4 ply	4 ply
Sport	Double knit	8 ply
Bulky	Chunky	10 ply

Crochet Hooks

US	METRIC (mm)
B	2
C	2.5
D	3
E	3.5
F	4
G	4.5
H	5
I	5.5
J	6
K	7
M	8
N	9
O	10
P	12
Q	15

Knitting Needles

US	Metric (mm)	OLD UK
0	2	14
1	2.25	13
-	2.5	-
2	2.75	12
-	3	11
3	3.25	10
4	3.5	-
5	3.75	9
6	4	8
7	4.5	7
8	5	6
9	5.5	5
10	6	4
10.5	6.5	3
-	7	2
-	7.5	1
11	8	0
13	9	00
15	10	000

Knitting lingo

K (or k) = knit

P (or p) = purl

st(s) = stitch(es)

st st = stockinette stitch/stocking stitch

    (k1 row, p1 row rep the 2 rows)

g-st = garter stitch (every row k)

sl = slip

ssk = slip, slip, knit (slip 2 consecutive sts then insert left needle back into the front of the 2 sts and k the two slipped sts together)—i.e. this forms a decrease

psso = pass slip stitch over

skpo = slip 1, knit 1 psso

lp(s) = loop(s)

tbl = through back loop

    (i.e. ktbl or k tbl = k next st through back loop)

yf = yarn forward (ie. yarn to the front)

yb = yarn back (ie. yarn to the back)

k-wise = knit wise (ie. as if to k st)

p-wise = purl wise (ie. as if to p st)

m1 = make 1 by picking up thread before next st and K into back of it

inc = increase

dec = decrease

cast off = bind off

beg = beginning

alt = alternate

foll = following

rnd = round

rep = repeat

patt = pattern

rem = remaining

cont = continue

cm = centimetre(s)

in = inch(es)

LH = left hand

RH = right hand

RS = right side

WS = wrong side

Crochet

US	UK	
sl st	sl st	slip stitch
ch	ch	chain
sc	dc	single crochet = UK double crochet
dc	tr	double crochet = UK treble
tr	dtr	treble = UK double treble

US terms used in patterns in this edition

TIP!
When in doubt, follow the metric sizes as they are the most accurate.

Yarn suppliers

Thank you to all the yarn companies who kindly gave us the means to make the projects in this book— where would we be without them? We tried to keep a list of all the different yarns for each pattern, but so many were changed and made up as they went along by so many different knitters it proved impossible to keep track. Still, the main thing is to be able to knit what you want out of anything you have available, so that's what we did!

Debbie Bliss and Sirdar yarns

Knitting Fever Inc

315 Bayview Avenue

Amityville, New York 11701

USA

Tel: 631-546-3600

Fax: 631-546-6871

www.knittingfever.com

Check the Internet to

find a store near you.

Rowan Yarns:

Rowan USA

Westminster Fibers

4 Townsend West

Unit 8

Nashua, NH 03063

USA

Tel: 800-445-9276

Fax: 603-886-1056

www.knitrowan.com

The world-wide-woolly-web

www.castoff.info

We had to put our site first, or course. Catch up with all the "knit happenings" in the UK. There is also a chat room to meet other knitters organizing their own clubs out and about.

www.handweaversstudio.co.uk

The Handweaver's studio is one of those well kept secrets of London, but well worth a trip if you are in the area. They stock yarns for all kinds of crafts, not just weaving, so you may find unexpected fibers for your stash.

www.ukhandknitting.com

This is the site of the British Handknitter's Confederation (BHKC). They are the representatives of most of the larger yarn companies in the UK and have an informative website including national events, patterns, and basic knitting and crochet instructions for beginners.

www.fabrications1.com

Fabrications is an independent gallery dedicated to contemporary textiles. Now also a shop "The Hagedashery" selling yarns and organizing workshops.

www.jklneedles.com

Unusual and hard-to-find needles, hooks, and other knitting supplies.

www.stitchnbitch.org

The home of Stitch 'n' Bitch Chicago. Link up to knitting circles and clubs in the US, UK, and internationally.

www.yarn.com

Yarns, kits, knitting tools, knitting courses, and classes.

www.rowanyarns.co.uk

Fantastic designs for garments and accessories from Rowan's designers, including international stockists.

www.kaleidoscopeyarns.com

Yarns, kits, and knitting accessories.

www.tkga.com

The Knitting Guild Association of America, featuring knitting events, classes, and links to other organizations.

www.shetland-wool-brokers.zetnet.co.uk

Mail order specialist suppliers of Shetland Wool, yarn, lace, raw fleece, and hand-knitting accessories

www.theyarnco.com

New York knitting supplies company.

www.yarnsinternational.com

A wide selection of top quality yarn, with a full range of colors and weights.

www.sweetgrasswool.com

Stocking 100% pure wool grown in Montana from Targhee sheep fleece.

www.knitr2.com

Online magazine and stockist of unique yarns that can be knitted, tied, glued, written on, and stapled.

www.knitty.com

Canadian magazine full of original ideas and patterns, along with links to suppliers and knitting blogs.

www.loop.gb.com

A new yarn shop, due to open as we go to press, is always a cause of celebration. Loop, will be in Cross Street, Islington, London.

www.laughinghens.com

An online store for lovely yarns, and a forum for knitterly discussion as well.

www.dyedinthewool.co.uk

Fabulous natural yarns in colors that you won't see anywhere else.

www.texere.co.uk

Great for undyed yarns and bargains.

Acknowledgments

A book like *Knitorama* is a truely collaborative effort. Late night knitting parties, late lunches, and strong coffee to keep us all going, and of course, lashings of Yorkshire Tea throughout the days. Many heartfelt thanks to all those who made it all possible, from knitters, models, photographers et al.

* Hey Rachael, are we near the end now?

Models

Bows	Miss Harriet Vine
Garter	Miss Rosie Wolfenden
Duster glove	Mr Mark Pawson
Hand grenade	Mr Mark Pawson
Blindfold	Miss Rachael Matthews
Fried-egg earmuffs	Miss Annie Doi
Tea trolley	Miss Rachael Matthews
Dinnertime	Mr Yu Masui
Flying ducks	Mr Yu Masui
Hot water bottle cover	Mr Stephen Fowler
Speaker cover	Miss Amy Higgins
Flapper nightdress	Miss Naomi Johnstone
Gauge swatch Cardie	Miss Amy Higgins
Big-night-out bra	Miss Rachael Matthews
Patio Socks	Miss Annie Doi

AGGRESSIVE SCHOOL OF
CAST OFF
CULTURAL WORKERS

* Cast Off has been awarded this stamp in recognition of their unique and autonomous work in the field of creativity.

Thanks to the knitters

Naomi Johnstone: Nightdress, dishcloth, thong.
Sam Dickenson and Giulia di Patrizi: Bows.
Eithne Farry and Anna Wilkinson: Cardigan.
Joanna Wilkinson: Men's pants.
Katy Bevan: Knitted lingerie.
Tomoko Takahashi: Knitted cheese for sandwiches, silver speaker cable, stitching up the cardigan, much loved dinners, and encouragement.
Joy: Knitted ham for the sandwiches.
Flat B emergency knitters: Tetsujiro Kitazawa, Mai Kusumi, Maki Nakamura (sandwich bread through the night), Mika Uehara, Yuko.
My sister Charlie Worm: Big-night-out bra.
Rachael Matthews and Annie Doi: Everything else.

Thanks are also due to

Katy Bevan our wonderful ever-patient editor; *Annie Doi* for enormous things; *Amy Plant* for inspiration; *Azumi and David* for the vacuum cleaner; *Lucy Davidson* for Photoshop and picture sourcing; *Tatty Devine* – family; *Stephen Fowler* for various reasons; *BHKC* for yarn; *Sebastian Lowsley Williams* emergency masseur; *Taiko* for neighborly love; *Mark Pawson* – Director of the Agressive School of Cultural Workers; *DJ Squirrel Head*; and special thanks to all members of the *Cast Off Knitting Club* for boys and girls.

Other talents

Knitting design: Rachael Matthews and Annie Doi.
Photography: Angus Leadley Brown; additional shots Phil Wilkins; p.103 Cressida Pemberton Piggot.
Styling: Rachael Matthews, Annie Doi, and models' own.
Book design: Clare Barber.
Wooden buttons: David Matthews.

✻ *Yes, this is nearly the end. It is time to have a nice cool beer.*

Index